From Commerce, Oklahoma, to Yankee Stadium,

from a desperately poor boyhood to the very top of the world of sports—that's the story of Mickey Mantle, the Yankee slugger who has become a legend in his own time.

It's all here. Mickey's spectacular career in baseball, his victories and defeats, his memories of the magic years when the New York Yankees were a powerhouse no one could beat.

What's more, *The Education of a Baseball Player* is an education in the finer points of the game. *Your* game. This is a valuable collection of professional lessons from a star who learned them the hard way.

The Education of a Baseball Player
was originally published by Simon and Schuster.

Mickey Mantle

The Education of a Baseball Player

PUBLISHED BY POCKET BOOKS NEW YORK

THE EDUCATION OF A BASEBALL PLAYER

Simon and Schuster edition published September, 1967

A Pocket Book edition

1st printing........February, 1969
2nd printing.........March, 1969

This *Pocket Book* edition includes every word contained in the original, higher-priced edition. It is printed from brand-new plates made from completely reset, clear, easy-to-read type. *Pocket Book* editions are published by Pocket Books, a division of Simon & Schuster, Inc., 630 Fifth Avenue, New York, N.Y. 10020. Trademarks registered in the United States and other countries.

L

Standard Book Number: 671-77055-1.
Library of Congress Catalog Card Number: 67-22937.

This *Pocket Book* edition published by arrangement with Simon and Schuster.

Printed in the U.S.A.

To my wife, Merlyn, whose love, understanding, and devotion make everything else secondary.

M. M.

I am grateful to my friend Bob Smith not only for dragging this material out of me but for helping me put it into publishable form.

M. M.

CONTENTS

(Sixteen pages of photographs follow page 48.)

The Education of a Baseball Player

chapter one

When I was a boy in Commerce, Oklahoma, the very best place to play ball, except for the ball field where the Commerce Merchants played, was the "Alkali"—a flat stretch of plain where lead-mine shafts had been sunk and abandoned, and where chat-piles, heaps of exhausted ore, some higher than houses, made mile-long shadows in the early morning. The dry summer winds would sift the alkali dust from the tops of the chat-piles and sprinkle it over the plains all around, burning them bare of grass and undergrowth until the whole area was hard-packed and barren as a parade ground. The cave-ins and the old shafts, closed off by beaten fences any boy could climb over or through, created a constant hazard, yet it was not one that bore heavily on us. The bad feature of the place, to a boy playing ball, was the outfield, which went on and on, without a ditch, or a brook, or a fence, or an embankment, just flat plain that stretched unbroken to the back yards of Commerce. A ball hit over an outfielder's head meant a weary chase, for the hard ground would hardly slow the ball at all, and sometimes it would skip away faster than a boy could run, until it seemed bound to get back to his own back yard before he did.

I think that endless outfield is the chief reason why I became an infielder, despite my lack of aptitude for that job. When I got big enough to have some say where

I played, I refused to play outfield on the Alkali. When I was real small, but still able to play ball with my betters, I was not supposed to be out on the Alkali at all, and if my mother caught me there, as she did once or twice, she would haul me home and really warm my britches. People still told about children who had fallen into the cave-ins and been killed, but I had never known of any. Still, my mother was bound that none of her own young would tumble to an untimely death down one of those black holes. She did not object to my playing ball, however. On the contrary, she and my father agreed that there was nothing a growing boy could do better than play baseball as long as daylight would let him. There were days when I left home with nothing more than a Thermos jug of water, to play ball from breakfast until dark, without even a break for food, and my parents sent me off with their blessing.

Baseball had long been my father's passion. He named me—his oldest—after a baseball hero of his own, Mickey Cochrane, and my name was always Mickey, not Michael, just Mickey. All his youth my father had wanted to be a professional baseball player, and like my grandfather, Charles Mantle, he had played amateur and semi-pro ball throughout our corner of the state. While his aim had always been to play shortstop, he was best at pitching and when he did not pitch, he played the outfield. He never wanted to sit on the bench. So it happened that my father, who was known everywhere as Mutt Mantle, although his name was Elven, decided that if he couldn't become a professional baseball player, I should. He was almost comic in his determination to make a baseball player out of his little boy. When I was still in the cradle, I had a knitted baseball cap; and a pair of his old baseball pants were whittled down to fit me before I was in kindergarten. I believe too that he put a baseball and a glove in my crib when I was still too new to do much more than chew at them. It was a wonder, I suppose, that I did not turn against baseball, from having it forced on me so young. But instead I loved the game with a fierce devotion that has never slackened. Once I had learned to hit a ball with a bat, I needed none of my father's urging to play the game. Knowing that it pleased my father to see me do well at the game only made it twice as much fun to me.

No boy, I think, ever loved his father more than I did. I was a good boy, really, who needed little disciplining, and I would do nearly anything to keep my father happy. He was a big, strong, stern-looking man, just a fraction short of six feet tall, lean and well muscled, with the strong, gnarled hands of a miner, and dark, thick hair, a good-looking man and a good athlete. He was only nineteen when I was born and he died when he was just past forty, so I never knew him except as a young and vigorous man, basically, and a loving, generous parent. He never had to raise his hand to me to make me obey, for I needed only a sharp look and a word from him and the knowledge that I had displeased him to make me go and do better.

He never drove me to play baseball, for no one ever had to do that. But he worked hard to help me improve and he gave me good advice to follow and played with me when he had the chance. It wasn't the thought of riches or fame that drove me. I didn't think about those things. I had no desire to leave home or to get very far from Commerce and the towns around us. What did keep me driving hard, from the time that I was ten, to hit the ball better and farther was first of all my own love for the game and then my love for my father. I knew from the time I was small that every small victory I won, and every solid hit I made or prize I was awarded, brought real joy to my father's heart. Not long ago, when I read in the paper that George Scott of the Boston Red Sox had telephoned his mother to tell her of being chosen for the All Star team, I felt a tingle of sympathy. And when I got on first base against the Red Sox that day and had a chance to talk to George, I mentioned this to him and we agreed that having someone to share an accomplishment with, someone you knew would get a thrill from it, made the accomplishment twice as sweet.

When I first started to play games with a bat and ball, I was about eight or nine and my playground was our own back yard. With my two little friends, LeRoy and Nick, I used to engage in a game that I think was probably familiar to kids all over the country in those years—the time just before the Second World War began. All the game required was a bat of some kind, a tennis ball, and three boys—one to pitch, one to bat, and one to field the ball. Each of us would take on the name of a favorite team (mine was always the New York Yankees) and we would stay at bat right through the whole line-up, or until three men had made out through having fly balls caught. I would be Charley Keller, and Frank Crosetti, and Joe DiMaggio, and Joe Gordon, and Red Rolfe, batting right-handed or left-handed, according to how the men themselves stood at the plate. If I was DiMaggio, I batted right-handed. If I was Tommy Henrich, I batted left. And that was where I got my first practice at switch-hitting, before I was ten years old.

The bats we used were bats that had been given us by grown-ups, or discarded by the local town team. To fix them so that we could swing them freely, we would saw several inches off the barrel. In those days there was no Little League promotion to fill the stores with kid-sized equipment. Even if there had been, I don't believe we could have afforded it. For a long time we played with just any sort of paraphernalia we could find.

In our back-yard game, hitting was everything. A ball that went over the roof of the house was a home run. If it landed on the roof, it was a triple, and shorter hits were doubles or singles. A caught fly was out. We would keep track of the men on base and the scores, from inning to inning and game to game. We would figure out the "league standings" of the teams we represented and keep the records all season long to see which club won the championship. I don't recollect that I was any better at the game than Nick and LeRoy. The difference was—and the difference between me and many other boys who played ball with just as much skill—is that I had a father to encourage and push me. My father approved of my switch-hitting and urged me to keep at it. My grandfather was a lefty and my father threw right-handed and they would take turns pitching to me when I grew a little bigger, so I could get the practice I needed. For a long time it was awkward and difficult for me to bat left-handed, but my father would not let me quit. Some day, he said, baseball managers are going to use right-handed batters entirely against left-handed pitchers, then change their line-ups to use lefties against righties. You'll get to bat more often if you learn to bat from both sides, he told me, and of course, he was right.

Left-handed pitchers were almost as scarce as sea food out in that country in those days and I found myself—once I started playing team baseball—batting left-handed most of the time. It never seemed wholly comfortable to me and I still think I am better right-handed than left, assuming my legs are equally strong. If my father was not nearby, I would often sneak around and bat right-handed against a right-handed pitcher. Once he saw me do this and he called me off the diamond and sent me back home to get out of my baseball suit and stay home all day. After that, as long as he had his eye on me, I was a switch-hitter, and this is about the best thing that ever happened to me as a ballplayer. A switch-hitter never has to fret about a cross-fire pitch. If the ball is coming at you, it's going to hit you, for the curve ball always breaks your way.

In odd moments, when there was no ball game on, and when my grandfather was no longer there to pitch lefty, I played pepper games with my father and in those games I always batted left-handed. This is a habit that has stuck to me—batting left-handed in pepper games.

In the games I played with Nick and LeRoy in the Mantle back yard there was no base-running, and pitching was just tossing the tennis ball up to be hit. Hitting was the whole game. We had plenty of practice swinging for distance with our sawed-off bats, swinging free and easy, with no fear of getting hit by the ball and with plenty of time to wait for the pitch that looked right.

While both my playmates were just as good as I was at the bat, there was one game I could always beat them in. That was running. Right from my earliest boyhood I could run like a jack rabbit, and when I had most of my growth, about age fourteen, there was not a boy or man in town, and not too many rabbits, who could outrun me. My father had always been a good runner too and when he was in his thirties he still liked to think of himself as a sprinter.

We lived for a while in a small village called White Bird, just outside of Commerce, in a house befitting my father's job as ground boss in the Eagle-Picher lead and zinc mines, a job that paid $75 a week, fairly good pay in those times, but not riches by any means, especially with five strong kids to feed and buy shoes for. Our house stood some hundred yards off the highway on a gravel side road that led down from the mailbox. Evenings, after I had finished playing ball, I used to like most to go and wait for my father at the mailbox and walk with him down to our door. He would arrive in his heavy "safety" shoes, with steel toes and heels, and sometimes I would take his lunch box away from him and carry it as I walked by his side. One evening we talked about running. Maybe I had won a race that day and was boasting about it. Whatever it was, before we were half-way home he decided to take some of the brag out of me by racing me the distance from the mailbox. So back we went and off came his heavy shoes. In his bare feet, on that rough gravel, he sprinted that hundred yards to the house and I just outran him by a stride.

Like all good fathers, he had let me beat him in friendly matches when I was tiny, but once I had grown man-size, he treated me like a man, and made no allowances. I was fourteen when we raced that day and he was thirty-three.

It may have been that year, or the year after, that I received the Christmas present I will remember all my life. Christmas was always a thrilling day in our house, as in most homes thereabouts, for even though money was scarce, my father saw to it that Santa Claus forgot no one and he tried hard always to surprise us with things we longed for. The family was up early on Christmas morning, usually before it was full day, to see what lay under the tree. This morning my present took my breath away. It was a full-size professional model baseball glove, carrying Marty Marion's autograph, the best glove money could buy. I knew exactly what it cost, for I had yearned after it for a long time—it was $22, about one-third of my father's weekly salary—and I knew, as all poor boys do, exactly what that amount of money meant in a family like ours. Of course, I doted on the glove with an unholy passion, loving even the smell of it, and I caressed and cared for it through the winter as if it had been a holy relic. But most of all, my heart was bursting with the realization of what a sacrifice like this said about my father's love for me and about his pride in my ability.

By that time I had been playing for some time with boys older than myself and playing well enough to be picked no later than second when sides were chosen. The games we played when school was over were the same as boys still play everywhere. When there were not boys enough to complete two sides, we played "work-up," a game known in other parts of the country as "scrub," in which the last man to enter the game would start in the outfield and, as batters made out, work his way up to infield, pitcher, catcher and finally batter. There was usually just one base, and the batter had to run there and back on his hit. He stayed at bat as long as he could hit safely. When he went out, he started in the outfield once more. When we played sides, we chose up by "crow-nips," the ancient method in which a tossed bat is grabbed by one captain in one hand. Then he and the opposing captain take hold of the bat alternately, one boy's hand on top of the other, until there is no more room for a full set of fingers. If the boy whose turn it is to grip the bat can then take the knob of the bat in the tips of his fingers solidly enough to keep hold of it while he swings it around, he gets to choose first. We would play this game sometimes on a pasture, with cowdung, dried stiff as a shingle in the Oklahoma sun, for bases and sometimes a broomstick or a bedpost for a bat. Or if we were playing more formally, we might rig a backstop on the Alkali or in a vacant lot and use folded feed bags, nailed to the hard ground, for bases and a short board for the pitcher's mound.

One day we had nothing for a bat but a metal bedpost and I, playing catcher, and leaping too suddenly out to grab a pitch and throw out a man stealing, took the bedpost right in the back of the skull. I was laid cold for an instant—my first serious baseball injury—but I was up and back in the game before the pitcher had even cooled off.

I played on the Pee Wee baseball team as catcher, pitcher, and shortstop, and I tried other sports as well, both in school and out. My speed served me well in both football and basketball and I was the fastest runner in high school. I loved football and played it well. But in other sports I did not have the same desire to excel that I had in baseball, the only sport that owned my father's full devotion. Nor did I ever have in those sports the love of the game that you need to keep you playing it in spite of discouragement, hunger, pain, or darkness. There was one sport, however, in which I was a dead loss—swimming. I never did learn to swim, even though I often traveled with my playmates to the swimming hole in the Neosho River and always tried to stay with them when they went out to the sand bar to practice diving off an old log that had been stranded there. As a matter of fact, I came as close as any boy needs to, to losing my life in the river one day, and all because of shame. I used to make my way to the sand bar by wading out as far as I could in the deepening water, then shoving myself off from the bottom and floating face down until my mates were able to grab my outstretched hands and haul me up. One day just after I had dragged my naked self safely aboard the log, we spotted a woman standing on the far shore. Sudden panic overcame us, for we all stood there in our skin and we were all well-brought-up boys. My friends, almost as one, plunged wildly into the water, head first. Without thinking, so did I, and stayed down longer than I expected. I came up in water far over my head, sputtering, splashing, and gripped with sudden fear that shortened my breath even more. I took aboard a big gulp of river water and could not stay afloat. The water seared my nostrils, choked me, and burned my eyes, and I gagged desperately, trying for a breath. I sank deep into the murky water, with the slow current enfolding me and drawing me gently downstream. It was terrible to reach up for air and find only the warm river. At just what point the frantic hands grabbed me I do not know, for I came to as I was being dragged up on the bank, wretchedly sick, and spewing out river water in quarts.

That experience was probably what kept me from learning to swim, for it made me leery of trusting myself in deep water. Getting hurt at baseball never kept me out of the game, however, until the day when they had to carry me off the field. Bumps and bruises, cracked fingers or fat lips, bloody noses and small cuts—these never slowed me down. They could never get me off the diamond when I still had my bats coming to me. Hitting was pretty nearly all of baseball to me. Anyone could learn to field and run. It was hitting that won the game.

Looking back on it now, I don't believe I was even the best batter in town when I was a schoolboy. I had some playmates who seemed to me much better ballplayers—Bill Moseley for instance, who became the head coach at Topeka. Bill, incidentally, was the football player I liked to pattern myself after. Or at least he showed me a style of play that appealed to me, for he played like a madman, going all out at every chance, never giving up until he was gang-tackled and immobile, giving the game his full mind and full heart all the time he was on the field. I tried to do the same, and discovered it actually multiplied the fun of the game to immerse yourself in it this way.

But to get back to baseball: I actually considered myself the worst player of the lot I played with as a kid because my fielding were always erratic. But as I said before, I was the one who had the father to coach, encourage, and keep me playing. If there were no games going, or no other boys around with time to play, I would have those pepper games, with my father batting the ball on the ground as I tossed it to him, then knocking it right back when I fielded it and tossed it up again. I became an expert at this game and could go for an hour or more without booting a ground ball, while my father tirelessly tapped them down.

Our high school team did not amount to much and of course the season was short. But there were teams of all sorts to play on, once I was big enough. After the Pee Wee League there was the Gabby Street League, and then the Ban Johnson League with teams in most of the nearby small towns, in our corner of Oklahoma and in the neighboring corners of Kansas and Missouri. I played with teams from Picher and Douthat, Oklahoma, then for Miami, in the Ban Johnson League, and eventually joined the fastest teen-age team in the area—the Whiz Kids from Baxter Springs, Kansas. It was with the Whiz Kids that I began to make myself known beyond the columns of the local press. And when I was with the Whiz Kids, I very nearly became a pro before I meant to.

We had a really fine ball park at Baxter Springs, better than many I saw in the minor leagues, with good lights for night games and a clean grandstand. A river ran through the outfield, marking its outer boundary. In right field the stream was some 500 feet away, then a sudden bend brought it across center field about a hundred feet closer to the plate. No one in any club in the league had ever put a ball in the water, nor did it seem likely that anyone ever would. But one day I was feeling especially confident and strong and I stepped to the plate each time feeling sure I was going to break a baseball in two. The first time up I caught a good pitch and put it far out over the fielder's head in right center. The next time I drove another one up the same alley. The third time I landed a ball plunk in the flowing water, 400 feet away. By this time the loyal fans were almost hysterical. They were all on their feet, and all screaming as I jogged home. It was more applause than I had ever heard in my life and it seemed to tighten all the skin on my chest and neck. I took off my cap to the crowd and submitted to the pummeling and hand-shaking of all my teammates. Then someone in the stands took it on himself to start passing a straw hat around for contributions in my behalf. After the game the man came down and handed me $54. I was ready to burst with happiness by then and I know I could do no more than grin happily at the man and tell him thank you a dozen times. That was the largest amount of money I had ever had all to myself at one time in all my young life, and my father and mother made no attempt to interfere with my spending of it. But when school opened in the fall, I found myself barred from football and basketball. Accepting the cash, according to the school authorities, had somehow turned me into a professional. So I had to scratch up all the money again, by doing odd jobs, until I had turned the whole $54 back to the man to be redistributed. I don't recall who got it finally, but I know it was a bitter task for me and one I brooded over for a long time. In those days $54 to me seemed like a half interest in a gold mine.

In all other ways but money, however, I acted the part of a pro while I was with the Whiz Kids. Pride in my club, in my uniform, and in my position with the team helped make a better ballplayer out of me. My mother, who was a devoted, or even a rabid, fan of the game, used to alter my uniforms to give them an even more professional cast. I liked the pants snug and she made them that way. Unlike the rest of the boys at that time,

I did not favor the Lefty Gomez style in pants. I did not want them to stretch almost to my ankle, but just to cover my knee. This meant that my poor, patient mother had to add extra inches to the uniform stockings so that they would meet the bottoms of the pant-legs. But she performed this task eagerly, with as much concern as I had that I should look the part of a real ballplayer.

Boss of the Whiz Kids was an open-hearted and open-handed man about as big as a doorway. This was Barney Barnett, who looked like one of those big old Dutchmen that every small town seemed to own one of. He had a good-natured, easy-to-take-to face and a warm, friendly manner. He liked kids, loved baseball, devoted every spare moment to coaching and promoting the game, and counted himself lucky to come out even at the season's end. When he was younger and weighed somewhat less than the 275 pounds he toted around at this time, he had played semi-pro baseball all around the neighborhood, as my father had. Like my father, Barney was a ground boss in the mines and he was no richer than any of us. In everything but money, however, Barney was a millionaire. He was vastly happy in his promotions, a welcome figure all over that part of the world, an active part of a baseball game nearly every day through the summer, and the acknowledged leader and adviser of a swarm of healthy and rambunctious boys, who all would have voted for him for president. Barney knew a great deal about baseball too, just as my father did. Most of the fundamentals of the game—those odds and ends of tactics that eventually become second nature—I learned from Barney and my father.

One of the things I recall best about Little Barney (he had a son called Big Barney because he was a few inches taller than his dad) was the party he gave each season to celebrate the arrival of the new uniforms. Then we would all gather from the nearby towns (Commerce was sixteen miles from Baxter Springs) to meet at Barney's house to gloat over our new garments, and to consume all the Cokes and ice cream and sandwiches we could hold. Barney was an unselfish, outgoing man, like a thousand other small-town promoters. I wish someday there could be a Hall of Fame to memorialize all the Barney Barnetts of the land, who really keep baseball alive in the country and teach youngsters to share their love of the game.

Of course, there were many other amateur ball clubs in and around Commerce and I played for a number of them. When I was still in my early teens, I played now and then for the Commerce Merchants, the town team, peopled mostly by local fellows in their twenties and thirties. And when I was not filling in at shortstop for them, I might be shagging foul balls behind the backstop or out in the bare reaches of the outfield.

My father's home town was Spavinaw, Oklahoma. This is where I was born and where many of my father's kinfolk still lived. Every Sunday the Spavinaw town team used to play the team from Salina or another small town and my father would carry the whole family down to see the game—my poor sister protesting most of the way. My father would play in the outfield, and when I was big enough, I was allowed to play shortstop. This was real old sandlot baseball, the kind so many kids are brought up on, with haphazard equipment, and well-worn gloves, bats of every vintage and color, and often a straw-hatted umpire who had a hard time covering all the plays. Kids would romp in the outfield and spectators would sometimes move down close to the baselines to yell encouragement. The smell of dry grass and slow-settling dust, of sweat and leather and new baseballs, the singsong yelping of the infield, the feeling of comradeship as you sat bunched tight with your teammates on the splintery old bench and hooted at the opposing pitcher—these were all as much a part of the game as anything you did on the field.

There was always high feeling at these games and a fierce desire to win. Often there would be four Mantles on the Spavinaw team, with a dozen others in the stands to yell for us. The infield was rough as a gravel road and the outfield in the far edges had grass deep enough to lose a baseball in. There were always Indians at these games, leathery young fellows just off the reservation who would invariably get drunk enough, about the seventh inning, to start throwing rocks at automobiles. Sometimes my father would pitch one of these games, with me right behind him to urge him to make a hitter out of some hayseed from Salina, and then my heart would really be full.

By this time in my life my father had stopped making any allowances for my youth and would bust his gut to make me try my utmost. He was not given to larding me with praise either, although I knew well enough how proud he was of me, especially when he could bring me down to Spavinaw and show me off to the kinfolk. But when the game was over, he would be the first to tell me how I had misplayed a ball and why, and to urge me for the hundredth time to learn to get my head down when fielding a ground ball. If I hit a home run in the game, I might see him standing there applauding, and he would shake my hand, as the others did, when I came back to the bench. But after the game, the home run would never be mentioned—just the errors.

Baxter Springs, Spavinaw, Picher, Douthat, Commerce, Miami—these towns made up all my baseball world in those days and I really had no immediate urge to play anywhere else. Of course, I had a dream of the big leagues, but that was like getting out of school, or getting married, or getting rich—just something that belonged to a faraway tomorrow. It seemed to me that I played baseball in every open spot in the area, on the Alkali, in pastures, in back yards, in Barney Barnett's fine field, in the local ball park, on the school ground, in the sandlot at Spavinaw, and in a dozen small towns within a twenty-five-mile radius. And all the time I was learning baseball, learning how to get a freer and more comfortable swing, to tag bases on the inside, to run the third-base line in foul ground, to charge ground balls, to wait out a pitcher, to get a jump on the pitcher to steal a base, and a dozen other simple acts that to a professional baseball player are as natural as putting butter on bread.

Among the things I taught myself was how to drag a bunt, and I learned that out of desperation. When I was playing in the Gabby Street League, a league for youngsters, the club from Treece, Kansas, had an overgrown pitcher called Long John Blair. He could really smoke that ball into the plate, in a way that scared most of us. He was bigger and stronger than any of us, although he was only in his teens, just one of those big old long-legged kids that seem to get their growth early. None of us would get a hit off him, unless by accident, and this really ate into my soul, because hitting was my pride.

I made up my mind finally that if I ever beat out old Long John, it would have to be on my speed. I didn't care how long his legs were. I knew he couldn't outrun me. So the next time we played Treece, I stepped up against Long John full of determination. I cut the air viciously with my bat a few times and dug in with my hind foot, making my usual preparations to drive the ball out of sight. I was batting left-handed, so the first baseman and the second baseman were both well behind the baseline.

Long John cranked up disdainfully and whistled that fast ball down. But this time, just as he let go, I took a few steps out to meet the ball, sliding my left hand up on the bat as I moved. Then I caught the ball in mid-flight on the fat part of the bat, just tapping it gently toward the second baseman. Luckily I had gauged it just right and the ball skipped along well to Long John's left. He sprinted out after it, but all he could do was wave at it with his glove, while I scooted down the line toward first. The first baseman had started for the ball too, so Long John kept right on going to the base. But I was there ahead of him, and there was no play made on me at all.

After that I nicked Long John for my share of base-hits, always in the same way. He knew what I was going to do, but his fielders never quite dared to play me to bunt, particularly as I always took my regular stance and swung my bat as if I meant this time to splatter the ball right into their faces.

By the time I was in my mid-teens, baseball was so much a part of my life that I had a hard time believing there was anything much else. When I wasn't playing baseball myself—and I played some form of ball every waking hour when rain or snow or cold did not prevent it—I was reading about baseball or watching it, or shagging stray baseballs at the local field.

Like all boys my age I knew the names and faces and even the batting averages of all the top players in both major leagues. My father and mother shared most of my enthusiasms, but the rest of the family were not always a hundred per cent pro-baseball. My sister Barbara, who had spent many an unhappy Sunday sitting on rock-hard seats at the Spavinaw baseball park, watching games that she could never understand, developed a real aversion to the game, of the sort some kids harbor toward books or figures when they are force-fed to them early.

My brothers Ray and Roy, the twins, enjoyed baseball and became good players. Ray, a left-handed batter, once led the rookie league and Roy, the right-hander, was top batter for his army team. They were both better-rounded athletes than I, and starred in school at basketball and football, as well as baseball. If my father had lived to work with them and encourage them, I am sure both would have made the majors. But neither one had the single-minded drive that was my heritage. When they were small, I used to use them to throw me practice pitches and chase the balls I hit, and sometimes when they rebelled, I would try to get my mother to tell them they *had* to play with me. My mother was always in favor of baseball but she refused to turn the twins into my private caddies, which I think was a good thing for all of us.

When the twins had got their growth, and I had gone away to be a baseball star, there was always a sort of rivalry among us. Every time I came home, it was necessary for me to trim them both in a foot race, just to prove to the neighbors that Ray and Roy, good as they had grown, were not yet quite up to big brother. The smallest brother, Butch, ten years behind me, became a basketball star in school and a great ball carrier in football. But for me, it was baseball from the day the ground thawed until it froze up solid again.

Every now and then through the summer, when he had saved up money enough and could round up his companions, my father and one or two of his friends would schedule a pilgrimage to St. Louis to watch the Cardinals in a Saturday night game and a Sunday double-header. This, to me, was like a journey to the Big Rock Candy Mountain. It meant an early bath on Saturday, then getting into a clean T-shirt, clean blue jeans, and my beloved baseball cap, then a long humming ride, with my eyes wide open, my young mouth tight shut, all the way to the biggest city I had ever known: St. Louis, on the mile-wide Mississippi, where fabled characters in baseball clothes performed on a diamond that looked like a picture postcard.

That baseball cap, incidentally, was one of my deepest vanities. I used to labor to bend the hard visor into the curve that was the current style, so as to make me, I fondly hoped, look like an old hand at the game. I would have worn that cap to bed, I believe, if my mother had let me, and I often put it on first thing in the morning.

In St. Louis, after we had watched the night game, one of the men would buy a bottle of whiskey and, all five of us in two hotel rooms, we would sit and talk baseball until sleep overcame me. Even now I recall the bliss that visited me, to drowse off with talk of Stan Musial and Enos Slaughter and Marty Marion blending like music into my dreams. In the morning, we would always eat breakfast at the Fairgrounds Hotel, where the ballplayers were to be seen, bigger than ever they looked on the field, bronzed and alive and close by, so I could have talked to them if my father and my own shyness had allowed it. But my father was opposed to anyone's intruding on a famous person's privacy and he would never have stood for any of us to walk up unknown to a ballplayer and ask for an autograph. I doubt anyway if I could have found the courage, or even the voice, to speak unprompted to these living heroes. So I would just sit there and forget my griddle cakes and stare at Marty Marion or Stan Musial and give thanks that I had ever been so lucky as to sit close to men like these.

On Sunday, we would devote ourselves to the double-header and lunch on hot dogs, then tool home through the twilight, as happy as men and boys are ever given to be. It was 300 miles from St. Louis, across the whole width of Missouri, and it would be late night when we reached White Bird and I would already be half asleep.

I suppose I must have learned some baseball from watching these great men play, but I never consciously studied them. Hitting by now "came natural" to me and hardly a game went by that did not see me hit a baseball hard enough to send it clear to the fence, if not over it. Naturally, from traveling with the Whiz Kids, and getting my exploits written about in papers all through the area, I began to develop a growing reputation and once or twice during a game I was told in reverent tones that a big league scout was watching me. Such news never made any difference in the way I played. I was always in a ball game with all my heart, scheming, watching, studying, yearning for the right pitch, grabbing any chance to steal an unwatched base, so once the game began, it mattered not to me *who* sat in the stands—except if my father was there I knew I dare not bat right-handed against a right-handed pitcher.

One night when I hit especially hard for the Baxter Springs Whiz Kids, I knew that Tom Greenwade, the Yankee scout, was in the stands. As a matter of fact, that was to have been my graduation night at Commerce High and I had been permitted to get my diploma during the day, just so I could play in this game before Greenwade. But I knew I would have hit those balls just as hard if Greenwade had been 500 miles away.

My father, by that time, was doing his best to get me a big league trial. He had even carted me to St. Louis to try to get me a tryout with the Browns, but they were not interested in kid shortstops at all. The first major league scout to approach me, as it turned out, was a fellow well known in the area, Runt Marr, who scouted for the Cardinals. He came to my house one day and asked me simply not to sign with any other club until he had a chance to make me an offer. This put a chill of excitement into my bones but when days went by with no further word from him, I concluded there was not going to be any offer at all from that quarter.

My fielding, I knew, was often sorry. I had learned to charge a ground ball well, and if I could get an angle on a ball, I could field it cleanly and get off a fast throw. My arm was unusually strong and my throws would really hum across the diamond. But when a ball came straight at me, I was often undone. Somehow it was almost impossible for me to judge the speed or the bounce of a ground ball like that. I might back off foolishly, letting the ball play me, and then lose it altogether. Or I would turn my head as it reached me and the ball would skip by or bounce right into my face. I carried around uncounted fat lips in that day from stopping ground balls with my mouth. And the more often I got hit, the more I would shy at such a ball. Even the balls I fielded cleanly did not always mean an out, for I had a habit of rejoicing so in the strength of my arm that I would not take the time to get a sure eye on the target. I would just let fly with my full strength, and often the ball would sail untouched into the stands.

But my hitting just seemed to get better, and my speed on drag bunts made it possible for me to pull myself out of a batting slump by legging out a few base-hits almost any time I needed them. I doted on fast balls. Curves did not bother me but it was just that I could get better distance on a fast ball, and when I was ahead of the pitcher and knew he would have to come in with a fast ball, I could really bust it into small pieces. This was what my local reputation was based on, and when scouts came to see me, they came to see me hit.

I had had my preview for Tom Greenwade and nothing happened. Then, on a sultry evening in 1949, Tom drove with my father to another Whiz Kid game. Rain cut the game short and I dashed through the downpour to Tom Greenwade's car, to find my father sitting there with Greenwade beside him. I climbed into the back seat and listened to the negotiations. I'm not going to say my heart was in my mouth, because I already knew Tom Greenwade had seen me at my best. But I was somewhat atremble inside all the same as I sat there in silence while the two men talked.

This was no "We'll call you later" deal. Greenwade was there to sign me to a contract. Once I understood that, I don't believe I'd have been distracted by a tornado, much less by the pelting of rain on the car roof. Greenwade was solemnly outlining to my father all the reasons why I probably would never make good in the majors: I was too small; my fielding was atrocious; nobody knew what I would look like against really good pitching. All in all, he insisted, it was a chancy thing. But the Yankees were willing to risk a *small* investment.

My father may have believed some of this but I did not —not about my being too small anyway. Phil Rizzuto was holding down the shortstop post with the Yankees at that time and it would have taken one and a half of him to match me in size. And I was confident that I was as strong as most big leaguers already. Still I listened respectfully, convinced that Mr. Greenwade really believed what he was saying, and conscious at least that my fielding was a long way from major league quality. My father agreed finally that $1,100 would be an appropriate bonus on such a doubtful prospect, plus a $400 fee for playing out the season in the minors, and he had me put my name, along with his, on the paper Tom Greenwade gave him. It was not until the signing was announced in the paper and I read Tom Greenwade's prediction that I would probably set records with the Yankees, equaling Ruth's and DiMaggio's, that I began to wonder if my father and I had been outslicked. Greenwade, by *his* account, had just been going through Oklahoma on his way to look over a *real* prospect, when he stopped to talk to us. I never did find out who that *real* prospect was.

But all this was no more than a passing irritation. Just the chance with the Yankees was all I wanted or felt I deserved. I never for one moment believed I would give Babe Ruth's records a run, or even come close to matching Joe DiMaggio, who was my own private hero. Greenwade assigned me at once to the Class D club in Independence, Missouri, of the K-O-M League, and after I had had a few days' orientation at the Yankee farm club in Joplin, my father set out to deliver my body to Independence.

This was the first time in my life I had left home to stay and I was not entirely easy in my mind about it. I was glad my father was going to drive me to Independence. It was just seventy miles away. But still, to be without my family, in a strange bed, with ballplayers all probably much abler and much older than I . . .

At Independence, we went together to find the manager of the ball club, Harry Craft. He greeted us in his hotel room, with shaving cream all over his face. Yet, despite his state of undress, he had the same stern dignity about him that my father had, and a way of carrying himself that told you here was a man of the kind you don't meet every day. He shook my hand pleasantly and let us sit down while he finished shaving.

"From now on," my father said, "Mr. Craft is your boss. I want you to do just as he tells you and pay attention to what he says, just as if I were saying it myself. And I want you to play this game just the way you would play it if I were here to watch you. And to act in every way just as if I were right handy." I promised that I would. For I was struck nearly dumb now with the solemnity of the occasion, being an obedient son and, at seventeen, young for my age, as many a small-town boy was in that day. Then my father shook hands and left me and promptly I felt the beginnings of that dreadful uneasiness that shy people suffer when left suddenly in strange surroundings with people they do not know. I did not know where I was to sleep or take my meals, or when, and could not shame myself by asking. For a long moment I did not want to play professional baseball at all, I just wanted to be home.

LESSON ONE

One trouble with me as a teacher is that I do not really believe that anyone can be taught to play baseball. You have to want to play, with all your heart, want to so badly that you will cut the grass and mark out a diamond, and shovel dirt, and go without food just to play the game. And of course you have to want to get better at it, so you can keep on playing it in any company. And you have to ignore bruises and bumps and cuts and defeats and errors, or at least forget about them.

What gives a person a drive like that I don't really know. With me I know that, besides my natural love of the game, I had a burning urge to please and impress my father. It was not that I had any fear of punishment. But perhaps I had caught a hint of his own deep disappointment in never having been more than a semi-pro, and I wanted to make it up to him somehow. There was nothing I would not have done to please him.

Other boys, I think, may just be driven by a need to catch up with bigger kids, or win their favor, and take part in their games. And some players have such a fever to be first in everything that they are on fire with it all the time. Whatever the motive may be, a ballplayer cannot do without it. There is endless fun in the game—at least for the first eight or ten years—but the desire for fun is not enough. You have to be ready to drive yourself, even to punish yourself, and to fight down every discouragement, to get better and better at the game.

Not that it is really all that grim. Satisfying an urge like that by playing a game you love is one of the highest forms of enjoyment.

As I pointed out in the narrative, I was not by any means the most gifted ballplayer among my playmates. But I had the urge, the opportunity, and the sort of father who could criticize and encourage you without scaring the hell out of you. So I kept on playing when the other fellows quit and I played baseball when they found other pastimes more persuasive. There was no Little League in those days, where parents could stand on the sidelines and scream at the umpires, but there was a Gabby Street League for the small boys and a Ban Johnson League for the older ones, those that wanted to play, and they operated on a big league basis.

I am all in favor of Little Leagues, naturally, for I want to see every kid given a chance to play. But I don't see what parents think they are accomplishing when they drive their kids to play baseball, and "coach" them by yelling at them for the things they do wrong. If a kid does not want to play baseball, he shouldn't play. My boys don't.

But if a boy wants to play, then he can learn by playing the game hard, by watching the older players, and by struggling to correct his own weaknesses, or finding a way to compensate for them—as I found the drag bunt would enable me to get hits off a pitcher who was too strong for me.

My idea of a ballplayer with the unquenchable desire to play was Hank Bauer. Hank was forever champing at the bit and he felt that the dirtiest trick any manager could pull on him was to leave him off the line-up card. Of course, Hank did get platooned, because he was not a switch-hitter, but he never fell asleep on the bench, because he always felt that Casey might relent and put him into the line-up. And when he did get in, he sometimes set the place on fire. He would run out a pop-fly as if it was a grounder to the shortstop, and he would make it his business to break up a double play any time he was on first and the batter hit into a force play.

Another roommate of mine, Billy Martin, had this fierce desire too, combined with a faith in his own ability that would really make you gasp. If he found himself batting number eight or even seven, he would turn on Casey Stengel with his eyes on fire. "What is this," he would demand, "a joke? Maybe I'll be hitting behind the bat boy next!" Casey would not give in to him, but he admired Billy for his spirit just the same.

Batting is the important part of the game. But I guess I have to confess I don't believe in batting coaches. If a boy understands what the object is—to hit a pitched ball hard and straight with the bat, or to put the ball where it cannot be promptly fielded—he will develop his own proper stance, his own most natural swing, and learn to hit all kinds of pitching. The number one consideration is to be *comfortable.* Do not pick out a bat because it has Mickey Mantle's name on it, or Willie Mays's, or Roberto Clemente's. Pick it out because you can handle it without any strain. A good many kids, probably urged by ambitious parents, or by a desire to grow up quickly, will use a bat they cannot even sustain the weight of. If you cannot hold the bat out straight in one hand, without having it droop or strain your wrist, then you should not pretend you are comfortable with it. Get one that fits your strength, no matter what it is and you'll outhit the kid that carries the war club to the plate and then cannot swing it level.

There are almost as many different stances as there are ballplayers, and you will find batting coaches to swear by them all. Some batters use an open stance, half facing the pitcher, the forward foot further from the plate than the hind foot, on the theory that this enables you to handle an inside pitch better. But Gene Woodling could slaughter an inside pitch from a wound-up crouch that made him look as if he were trying to hide.

Some batters keep their feet close together, in the Babe Ruth manner, because a long stride is supposed to give you more power. Ted Williams had one of the shortest batting strides known to man, and he never seemed short of power.

No, there is no perfect stance. Every batter is built differently, has his muscles distributed differently, and reacts with different speeds. You cannot even let someone else tell you where you must stand in the batter's box. As long as you can reach any part of the strike zone with your bat, you should stand where it seems most natural to stand. Rogers Hornsby, one of the game's greatest hitters, stood as far back in the box and as far away from the plate as the lines would allow him. Ty Cobb, who was probably the greatest (from what they tell me), crowded the plate close.

The hitter I most admired, Joe DiMaggio, also hit from a spread stance and took a stride that could be measured in inches. Yet he could power a ball out of the park, no matter where it was pitched. Sometimes I have seen him hit a ball that seemed to have gone by him, snapping those powerful wrists at the very last second. Yet, much as I admired him, I would never have been comfortable in that spread-legged stance. I would have felt handcuffed.

The one habit I learned, which may have contradicted this advice to be comfortable, was to hit from both sides of the plate. I never would have done that if my father had not been right at hand to keep me practicing it. But, as I said, it was a great thing for me. It enabled me to stay in the line-up against all sorts of pitching. And it enabled me to stand up to any pitch without fear that it might break away from me. If it was coming at me, I knew it was going to hit me, and I could bail out in plenty of time, without any danger that the ball would break over the plate and leave me looking foolish.

What made me a success at hitting was not what anyone taught me but what I taught myself in hours and hours of practice. Fortunately I was able to start early, developing the habit of swinging a bat to meet a thrown ball. It was a tennis ball I swung at, and a half-bat, or a stick that I swung, but that did not matter. I was still training my eyes and muscles to coordinate properly for the purpose of swatting a ball over the nearest roof. Of course, to be able to do this for days on end I needed understanding parents, who did not look on such activity as a waste of time for an eight-year-old.

There are some parents who are all in favor of having their sons play ball but who feel they can help them become expert at it only if they stand over them, teach them the "right" way to stand and to swing, supply them with official equipment, and correct every move they make. I swear I think that is probably the worst possible way to turn a boy into a ballplayer. It is more likely to turn him against baseball for life, for he will never get to know it as a game in which he can lose himself, which he can discover in his own way, and in which he can get better while actually having fun. It isn't the coaching and the correcting that counts; that can be poison to little kids, and may drive them right back to the comic books for recreation. Really small kids cannot play with a hard baseball or a full-size bat, and it isn't important that they do. What is important is that they discover baseball is fun—and that it gets to be more and more fun as you get better at it.

Of course, once I became addicted to the game, my father gave me a lot of help, first in just working out with me when there was no game going, and then in supplying hints about how to avoid errors and save time on the bases and such things. As for hitting, that soon became instinctive with me. I just seemed to have absorbed on my own all the teaching that a coach could supply. And I absorbed it by practice.

Base-running the same way. I enjoyed running so much that I wanted to steal a base every time there was one open, so I learned, through working at it, to recognize the telltale moves by a pitcher that meant he was really going to throw to the plate. And I learned naturally that you had to get a real good jump on the pitcher—to gamble that you were right about his being ready to throw to the plate—before you could steal a base.

There is one point about batting that even pros need to be reminded about sometimes and that is to keep the eye fixed on the ball. This is the very best habit you can develop, because all your training—to coordinate eye and muscle—will be thrown away if your eye wanders off the ball at the crucial moment, to pick out the spot where the ball is going to land, or to see how far it is going to travel. Ideally, you should see the bat meet the ball. I know people say that this is impossible, that the ball just travels too fast for your eye to stay with it. But I am not convinced. I still think you should watch that ball right into the bat, or right on past you if you are not going to swing. Watch it when the pitcher rubs it up, watch it when he takes the sign, watch it when he goes into his motion, watch it all the way down to the plate—and past it if you let it go.

Don't think that only amateurs forget to watch the ball. One day we beat the Dodgers because one of the finest hitters (and best fellows) I ever met, Roy Campanella, up at bat when a home run would have put the game on ice, turned to look at the distant left-field seats—and so missed the ball. He did it not just once, but several times, simply out of eagerness to go for the distance. I could hear people yelling to him to keep his head still, but Roy was smelling blood—Yankee blood—and he had no ears for the advice.

A sharp contrast to this was a hit Billy Martin made that won us a series against the Dodgers. Billy was no match for Roy Campanella in power, or in average. But he was a man you could count on in the clutch. In this game, I legged out a hit in the ninth that moved Bauer into scoring position. Then Billy came up. He made no effort to ride the ball into the seats. He just picked out his pitch and shot it right back through the middle, and the thing I remember about this hit is that when Billy connected, you could see his eyes sighting right down the bat at the ball. But Billy, when he got into the clubhouse, kept interrupting his own rejoicing to complain about a hit that he swore the official scorer had stolen from him. That was Billy, always wanting to do just a little better.

Bunting is one type of batting you are just not going to be able to do if you don't keep your eye fixed on that ball. Playing pepper games with my father, I did a lot of chopping and bunting, and I know this helped me in all my hitting. It taught me how best to hold the bat to get complete control of it and how to get the ball where I wanted it to go. In swinging freely, I never had any use for place-hitting, for going with the pitch, or any of that stuff. I swung to drive the ball as far as I could. But in bunting, I became pretty adept at tapping the ball with just the right amount of force to get it by the pitcher, without sending it all the way to the second baseman.

To bunt to get on, you have to conceal your purpose from the pitcher until the last moment, so he cannot come in so high that it is impossible to bunt. It is easy enough to do this when you have your eye on the ball, for you wait until that pitching hand comes around at the start of the pitch. Then you slide one or both hands up on the bat, so you can get better control, and meet the pitch with the fat part of the bat. A slight tap, with about the force you might use to tap a thick pane of glass without breaking it, is usually enough to send that ball past the pitcher before he can get over and handle it.

Drag bunts have to be performed by a left-handed batter, naturally, for the ball cannot be "dragged" from the right-hand side of the plate down the baseline. But a lot of batters think that the idea of a drag bunt is to start running toward the base before the pitch gets to the plate. The step you take however—with the left foot—is to bring you closer to the pitcher. You move right up in the batter's box. But you do not move out of it toward first, because you want your bat to cover the whole strike area. If you run away, trying to reach back to bunt the ball, you may leave half the plate uncovered and an outside pitch will be just a big strike.

I don't mean to say, however, that a right-handed batter cannot bunt to get on base. One of the classiest bunters I ever saw was Phil Rizzuto, a right-handed batter who could get such a start on a bunt that he was the equal of a left-hander. He would hold his regular stance at the plate and would seem to be starting a full swing. But he would slide his right hand up on the bat as it came level and would catch the ball right on the fat part of the bat. Actually his move was almost a chopping motion, to bring the bat level without swinging it around his body. He would pull his left elbow in tight as the bat came down and present the level bat to the pitch. His hind foot would come forward as he met the ball and he would be away before the ball hit the ground. It was really a delight to watch Phil do this—a delight to nearly everyone except the pitcher. I don't believe I have seen anyone, before or since, who could do it better.

Sacrifice bunts are not made with any effort to get on. But still it is just as well to conceal your aim, even if everybody feels pretty sure the situation calls for a bunt. There is no need to give the infielders any extra time to start toward the plate to field the ball.

Stand there as if you meant to take your regular cut, and then move into bunting position as the pitcher starts to bring the ball around or over in his final motion. Most good bunters perform the sacrifice bunt by turning to face the pitcher directly. You bring your hind foot up in the box—*never* move back—and slide the hand or hands up on the bat to shorten your grip on it. I don't believe it matters much if you bring both hands up together and present just the upper half of the bat to the ball, or if you slide one hand up to about the halfway point and present the whole bat. You do have to take care not to hold the bat too tightly or too loosely. If you grip it in a stiff, tight grip, the ball will rebound too sharply and may turn into a double play. If you hold it too loosely, the pitch may knock the bat out of your hands and all you'll have will be a foul strike.

I think the best way is to hold the bat back in your hands, not with the fingertips, but with the inner joints, and to keep your arms bent. If you get the bat about eye level, crouching to sight right over the bat, it will be easier to get the ball on the ground, and you can crouch right down to meet a low pitch. Stiff arms and straight-up stance usually mean pop-ups.

Most clubs go in for bunting practice but it is usually for pitchers, who are not expected to do much more than bunt when they go to the plate. But I think plenty of bunting practice is good for anyone. It is especially good for youngsters. It makes it easy for them to get in the habit of watching the ball right into the bat. And it also helps develop confidence, for nothing begets confidence more than the knowledge that you can *always* hit the ball, no matter who pitches it, or how, as long as it is in the strike zone.

Confidence is everything, in batting. Nobody is going to hit safely, except by blind luck, if he goes to the plate with the conviction that he is going to have a hard time hitting a certain pitcher. Practice, and more practice, teaches you that there are ways to make even the best pitchers throw you the pitch you want. And it is practice that teaches you that there are certain pitches you can always hit. If you go up to the plate looking for that pitch, and knowing you can belt it when it comes, you have gone halfway toward making yourself a good hitter.

Both Billy Martin and Bobby Richardson owned plenty of confidence, which was what made them so dangerous in a pinch. There was no pitcher living that either man believed he could not hit. Yet there could not have been two more contrasting types. Billy was aggressive, ebullient, often hollering. Bobby was quiet, steady, easygoing. But in each man you could just feel the confidence oozing.

There are base-running points that will save you time. But the most important aspects of running bases, you can learn only through practice as I did. I learned, for instance, that I could not wait for a coach to tell me whether I could make an extra base or not. I alone knew my own speed and momentum and if I watched the ball, I could judge better than anyone whether I could make it to the next base before the throw came in. Of course, I had to know something about the fielder's ability, and had to notice if the ball was going straight to him, or to his throwing side, or to his glove side. But if I waited to get a sign from the coach, I would have broken stride and lost momentum.

It helps though to have someone remind you to tag the inside corner of the bases, as a way of making the route shorter. And it is good to realize that, if you have decided to try for an extra base, you must make your swing *before* you get to base number one. Base-runners who advance from first to second by way of right field, or who go from third to home via the on-deck circle are the ones who slide into tag-outs. If you see that your hit is going to be good for two bases, you have to swing out before you reach first base, then run directly to second. Or if you decide while on second to try for home on a base-hit, you have to swing out as you approach third base, cut to the inside corner of the base, then sprint straight home.

Sliding was another thing that seemed to "come natural" to me, because I enjoyed doing it and kept at it until it was second nature. I always favored the "pull-up" slide, where you go in straight for the base, with one leg bent inwards at the knee, riding along on the knee and shin. This form enables you to come right to your feet and be ready to keep going in case of an overthrow or an outfield error. You do have to remember to keep your hands high on this slide and not to roll to one side or another. If you put your hands down, you can break a finger. And if you roll over to slide on a thigh, you almost automatically put a hand down. Some runners take dirt in both hands to remind themselves to hold their clenched hands up when they slide.

Really the best place to practice sliding is on a place where it is easy to do, and where you can taste the fun of it. Grass, even wet grass, is best for this because you slide easily, don't scrape your hide and are not so likely to snag a spike and get a foot twisted under you. (On the diamond you take care to turn those feet up, to avoid catching the spikes.) Once you catch on to the fact that the pull-up slide is really just a controlled fall, you will get a kick out of the practice, and it will become natural—as natural as sliding on wet grass.

Sliding is not just a way of avoiding a tag, although that is its main purpose. It is also done—although nobody ever seems to "coach" this—to break up a double play. Nobody in baseball goes out to hurt another player on purpose (unless there is some private grudge) but no club is going to win pennants if its players are reluctant to "take out" the pivot man so as to prevent a double play. In the big leagues the pivot man on a double play usually take the throw as he approaches the base, then tags the base as he steps across it to make the relay throw from the infield side. You have a right to the baseline and to the base and if you can time your slide to reach the base just as the pivot man gets there, or just as he turns to make the throw to first, you will most likely take his feet from under him, or cause him to leap high and make an off-target throw. This is legitimate baseball tactics and infielders expect it. Baserunners like Enos Slaughter or Hank Bauer would no more think of letting a pivot man get off a double-play throw unhindered than they would allow a fielder to push them off a base so he could tag them out. When you try to break up a double play this way, you are simply standing on your rights.

Twisted ankles are often caused by badly fitting shoes or by loose spike-plates. Never wear baseball shoes that are too big for you or that have stretched and become sloppy. Don't wear shoes with loose plates on them or anything flopping loose. Your baseball shoes should be a size smaller than your dress shoes. (I wear a size ten dress shoe and always get a size nine baseball shoe.) It is good to have a spare pair around to use for games while you have your old pair for practice. Every spring I get five pairs of new baseball shoes. I wear a pair left from last season to play in, and I gradually break in my new shoes in morning workouts. Some ballplayers let a fellow with smaller feet break in their shoes. When the shoes develop a little give, so they start to get loosened up on the man who is breaking them in, they are usually ready to fit the owner snugly, as they should.

I used to take about as tender care of my glove as any boy ever did, and I applied all the oils and saddle soaps and other junk that was supposed to keep it pliable and make it last. But this was really more of a loving ritual than a practical means of improving the glove. By the time I had become a pro, I had decided I did not want a soft glove because it would let a ball through, while a stiff-fingered glove would more likely stop the ball. So I gave up my boyhood winter pastime of oiling and caressing the glove. Instead I would sometimes actually dip the glove in water (what sacrilege!) to stiffen the leather. Gloves nowadays are a whole lot bigger than they were when I broke into the game and you depend on them ever more to keep a ball from getting by.

But more important than equipment, or coaching, or learned advice, or watching experts play the game is actual practice. Nearly every boy who grew into a star at baseball has spent far more than the usual number of hours playing the game or has practiced some specialty tirelessly when his playmates were finding their fun in other ways.

Of course, not every boy is lucky enough to have a yard to practice in or a garage roof to drive the ball over. But it really does not take much room to develop skill at hitting the ball. You don't even have to have a regulation bat or a baseball. One of those plastic bats and a little whiffle-ball that you can actually use in the house will give you the practice you need at hitting a moving round object with a stick. Or a broomstick and a tennis ball out on the street will give you practice just as valuable. You can even get along without the ball to develop at least part of the power you need. Some players hang up an old spare tire in the cellar, with a mark on it for a target, and whale away at that with a baseball bat. This does not give you proper practice at hitting a pitched ball, but it does develop your arms and shoulders and helps implant the aggressive attitude you need. Also you have the satisfaction of always hitting something with your bat, to keep you swinging.

And if you keep swinging, you will accomplish wonders. You'll even cure batting slumps.

chapter two

I suppose small-town kids who go away for the first time still get homesick. But I have never met anyone who was any homesicker than I was my first days in Independence. It was going to be worse later when I went up to the Yankees. But for a time I seriously thought I would give up the whole deal and go back to playing ball around Commerce. What helped me get over my gloom in Independence was the fact that I was among boys my own age, all of them friendly and eager to accept a new guy, if he could help them win ball games, and all of them looking to raise hell, kid-style, in their off-hours. By the beginning of the second week I was one of the boys and would not have wanted life any different.

We had a good club, and after a very unhappy start, I had a good season at bat. In the field I set new records for booting ground balls. My trouble was still with the ball that came right at me, with my temperament, which sometimes dumped me into despair, and with my throwing, which reached new heights of wildness. I think I was so often overexcited by fielding a ball cleanly that I could not hold myself in check long enough to take the range of the target. I was always throwing the ball as if I had but a split second to beat the runner, and as a result many an easy out became a two-bagger. But this did not happen often enough to do the club any real damage. We were winning about five games out of every six, spread-eagling the league as if the whole thing was a joke. And we toured the Kansas-Oklahoma-Missouri area like a pack of puppies.

Traveling was by bus and the buses were usually so full of frolic and wild laughter that the trips, which should have been a drag, sometimes seemed hardly long enough. The big deal in that era was water guns and every member of the club owned one, which he carefully loaded before every trip and then unloaded at haphazard intervals, trying always to hit the victim when he least looked for it, or from an unsuspected angle. Harry Craft had almost endless patience with our shenanigans, far more than we deserved, I think, and more, I am sure, than nine managers out of ten. But we were winning steadily and Harry, no doubt, was almost as merry at heart as we were on that account, and he knew he had a pack of adolescents in his care and realized that they responded best to a loose rein.

Every so often, however, the roughhousing would get out of hand. Someone would jump out of his seat to take vengeance on the wielder of a water pistol and attempt to wrestle the weapon away from him in the aisle as the bus rocked along. Then the yells would grow wilder and others would undertake to join the fray. At that point Harry would turn around from his front seat, half rising, and look us each in the eye. He might utter one phrase, like "Hold it!" But usually he just had to look and we would all grow silent and shamefaced and settle into our seats again. I never knew a man quite like him for making his will known with a single stern glance.

No one who traveled with us, however, or whose path crossed ours in Carthage or Bartlesville or Chanute or Ponca City or some other small town where we might sojourn, would have mistaken us for a chapter of the Christian Endeavor. The small hotels we put up at nearly exploded from the pressure of our monkeyshines. In that neighborhood in midsummer, melons were cheaper than chewing gum and we all used to carry melons to our rooms after supper. When we had eaten what we needed of them, and sometimes before we even bothered to bite into them, we would break them into handy sections for throwing at each other and would then carry our warfare out into the corridors, regardless of the protests of guests and management, and chase each other up and down through the creaky structure, with melon splattering on wall and door and head and body and protective arm until the place looked like the set for a Martin and Lewis comedy.

Of course, Harry Craft did not really tolerate such carryings-on and if they happened in his hearing, he would throw a halter on them. But usually he was off somewhere when the war began and he would hear of it only in the anguished protests of the hotel owner, who needed our custom badly, but not at the cost of all his other business. It was not always melon we made war with. Sometimes we would enliven the area by dropping bags filled with water out of the window, or take down the fire pails and lie in wait for someone walking down the stairs. Then we would douse him, or her, or them, without regard, and scamper into hiding with only our hysterical laughter and the screams of the victim to mark the deed.

This sort of endeavor was usually considered too extreme for passing off as mere boyish exuberance and after such an affray we sometimes found ourselves next day all lined up on the outfield grass, squatting on our haunches, to have our young ears scorched by a firm and low-voiced lecture from Harry Craft. Nobody wanted Harry mad at him and we all toed the mark when he gave us a hard look or a sharp reminder, so we would calm down for a day or two after being asked to remember that we were grown men now, and we would confine our roughhouse to the rooms.

The playing conditions, like the living conditions, on that Class D circuit were indeed fourth class. The infields were always skinned bare, except that there might be an occasional lonely tussock of wiry grass persisting where it could tip a ground ball out of line. There were small stones of all sizes on the baselines. Sometimes the outfield would end in a sharp embankment that promised a broken ankle to an outfielder who hit it unawares. The hot lights we played under called in mosquitoes nearly big and tough enough to carry a ballplayer off, and they would line up twelve abreast along our bare arms and sip our blood as we stood waiting for a play.

Crowds were often slender at our games but the fans who did show up were rabid enough to compensate for those that stayed home. Sometimes it seemed that nearly everyone in the stands had a dollar riding on the game, or on the inning, so frantic and so fevered did their pleadings become, and so wildly would they boo the umpires. But our fans were as happy as we were, for we hardly ever lost a game. And the players themselves, in minor league fashion, took as much open delight in our victories as any group of teen-age boys ever did. There may have been a few on that club who were over twenty, but they never revealed it by any of their actions. I suppose I was the youngest of all but in spite of what Mr. Greenwade had said, I was neither the smallest nor the weakest. I hit hard and often and made hay on the bases too. Playing only part of the season, I hit .313, made 7 home runs and drove in 63 runs while scoring 54. I also set some sort of record for errors, with 47 of them in 89 games—about one every other game. But at least I was spared those bumpy outfields and sudden dips and rises that can help make a ballplayer's life miserable in the bushes.

The off-season was a pleasant one. My bonus had allowed me to pay off the mortgage on the family home. I had some spending money left, a job in the mines when I wanted it, and a chance to play ball in the neighborhood when the weather allowed it. When the football season began, I went to see the high-school games, and in between times I attended to my glove and spikes as if they had been my pet cats. On Saturday after a football game I found myself on a double date with a friend of mine and I discovered I liked his date better than my own. But she was a pretty important girl in those parts and I was shy of her. Her name was Merlyn Johnson. She was a slim redhead, a majorette with the Picher High School band, and known all over the area for her lovely singing voice. I got a friend to intercede for me, and made a date with her on my own. After that we neither of us dated anyone else. My family was delighted with her, and my father began to talk about "a little redheaded grandson." (There was one eventually but my father was not there to hold him on his knee.)

In January, before the winds had even begun to grow warm again, I received a letter from Lee McPhail, director of the Yankee farm system, inviting me to attend their new rookie school to be held for the first time that year in Phoenix, Arizona. I was eighteen years old now and the end of the rainbow seemed almost in sight. But I was scared! Of course, I didn't expect to join the Yankees right away. But to get so close, so soon . . .

The Mantle family, except for the mortgage being paid off, had not spent a much more prosperous winter than usual. My father still earned $75 a week at the Blue Goose No. 1 mine of the Eagle-Picher Lead and Zinc Mining Company (he never made more than a hundred) and I was not about to tap him for the stiff price of a train ride to Phoenix. So I went to work in the mine with him, where I had spent short spells before, hoping to save, out of my $33 a week, money enough to get me to Phoenix and keep me there. My job was a sort of roustabout job, caddying for the men who kept the electric engines going, and the money mounted up very slowly indeed. We were deep into February with hardly any time left for rookie school and I still had not laid by enough to stake me properly, or even to get me to Phoenix clean and fed. As I fretted over this, I received a telephone call from George Weiss, general manager of the Yankees, asking why I hadn't appeared. I explained that I was still short of the fare and Weiss immediately sent me a ticket. I had not realized that big league ball clubs paid transportation.

My father and mother drove me down to Vinita, Oklahoma, to catch the express for Phoenix. I do believe it was one of the worst days in my life, when it should have been the gladdest. Somehow Independence had not seemed too far out of my own world. And all the time I was there, except for those first few days, I had felt at home with my teammates and especially with Harry Craft. But now—to abandon my home heath altogether—to get so far away that you could not even telephone without spending a dollar or more—to play ball with utter strangers, older men, hardened characters—not to know anybody at all—and to have my father so far out of reach! The thought had me talking nervously on the long drive to Vinita. In the station, waiting for the train to pull in, I kept swallowing hard and drinking more water than I ever needed before.

I knew I looked pale and frightened as I turned at the steps to the train, took my suitcase in my hand, and tried to say my goodbyes to my mother and father. I was just about able to speak. I got on the train, looked for a seat by the window where I could see my parents, and tried forlornly to smile as they waved up at me. The train began to roll at last and then the sobs rose up and choked me. For a whole hour I sat with my fist pressed tight to my mouth and my swimming eyes fastened unseeing on the blurred country outside as I tried to keep from weeping aloud. Tears kept welling up, in spite of me, and ran hot on my nose and cheeks. What a jerk I felt like! And how hard I tried to breathe deep and square up and look like a professional ballplayer. And how completely lost and woebegone I was! I wished I had never left home at all and could get off at the next stop and go back to my father and mother—and to Merlyn. Sometimes I would just whisper her name out loud to take my mind off my misery.

There was nothing in Phoenix to make me feel more cheerful or more at home. The hotel where they registered me was far bigger than any I had known on the Class D circuit; the help, I thought, more distant, and the appointments more overpowering. Although most of the other players were young too, and many of them no more sophisticated than I, I made no friends and shared their company only at the ball park. There I did well. In the thin air the baseballs would go rocketing off my bat like cannon shot and I put some drives farther away than I had ever hit before. My muscles were well tuned up by the hard labor in the mine. I worked religiously at every chore the coaches set, earnestly developed a sweat at calisthenics under the desert sun, ran like a mustang, swung the bat tirelessly, and did not even sulk at my errors.

No one was really unfriendly to me, either among the rookies, or among the regulars who were acting as instructors—until rookie school was called off because Commissioner Chandler felt that a few of the teachers in the school were actually cheating on the starting time by getting their own training started weeks early. The regulars had even less time for me than my fellow rookies had. I ate my meals glumly, answered when I was spoken to, holed up in my room alone in the evening, and kept asking at the desk for mail from home. It is hard for me now to convince myself that that was really me—bashful among strangers, hardly able to give my breakfast order to a waitress, and willing to spend night after night, in that warm and lively city, writing letters, reading western stories, or merely brooding in my room.

The other players all had their own friends to talk to and for all I knew may have thought me too surly to join them in their off-hour pastimes. One man I will always remember, however, as the first to show some real concern for me, and to make me feel as if I might not be wholly invisible and ignored. He was a lean, stern-looking man, nearly all bald under his baseball cap, with dark, deep-set eyes. Of course, I had known about him all my life but he seemed bigger and fiercer close up than in his pictures. He had a gentle voice and a handshake that was rough and strong as a miner's. This was Frank Crosetti, whom I came to know as Cro, and the only Yankee who has lasted all through my career. I called him Mr. Crosetti then, when he walked up and took my ball glove out of my hand. It was my precious Playmaker model, fingers slightly scuffed, pocket soiled and well broken in.

"Where the hell did you get this?" he demanded. "You can't field a ball with that. Get yourself a decent glove."

Somehow I managed to choke out a few words to make clear that I had no money for a new glove. I had no money, as a matter of fact, even for a phone call home. Cro shrugged and walked off. But the next day he handed me a fresh new glove of the style he used himself. It was a model that no store in Commerce could ever have afforded. I am sure Cro bought the glove with his own money but nowadays he pretends not even to remember it. It improved my fielding (and taught me the value of a fairly stiff-fingered glove) and it warmed my heart a good deal too. But it did not make me into a shortstop. Not even Casey Stengel could do that, as he was the first to realize.

The rookie school having been disbanded, with me scheduled to play with the Joplin Miners, the Yankees had no place to put me right away, so they packed me on a train for the longest trip of my life—all the way to Florida for some "conditioning" with the Kansas City club and, I suppose, a chance for some of the Yankee brass to size up their latest bargain. By the time I was finished there and had trekked back to Branson, Missouri, where the Yankees had a training camp for their lower farm clubs, all the homesickness had been scraped off me in the most painful way possible and I was beginning to feel a little like a man of the world.

Joplin was a Class C operation, with better pitching, a few more veteran players, and a higher salary limit—$3,400, pretty close to riches for playing ball all summer. But, of course, I was not earning the top salary. The best part of the move to me was not the few extra dollars but the fact that Harry Craft moved up too and right then he was the man, next to my father, whom I wanted most to be like. He taught me many things about baseball but he taught me many more things about being a man. I was impressed with the way he kept up his appearance, always wearing a necktie and a neat suit in the hotel lobby or on the street, and I never since have gone in much for walking into a dining room in a sweater. It seemed to me that Harry Craft always looked the part of a manager, or of a leader. He was friendly but dignified, stern but not sour, and he walked like a man who knew where he was going and what he was going to do when he got there. I can't say I patterned myself after Harry, for we are two very different people. But I looked up to him, enjoyed being in his company, and found myself imitating his manner of dress and public deportment occasionally, the way boys will when they find someone they admire.

I think my worst fault as a ballplayer, and one that even now I catch myself at and bawl myself out for, was getting down on myself, putting my head down and sinking into despair when I made an error (and I made plenty) or struck out (and I did that often). Harry got on me right away for this.

"Hold up your head!" he told me again and again. "You're not through yet!"

But this was a hard habit for me to beat. I suppose it must have had its origin in my strong desire to please my father when I was small, so that if I did something wrong, and something I thought would disappoint him, I would try to show right away that I was ashamed of it. Now, to please Harry Craft, I made a real effort to fight off this tendency to get down on myself and, after a brief sulk, I would usually be able to get back into the play.

One thing I began to notice was that, with somewhat better pitching, my hitting actually improved. There was such a thing, I discovered, as a pitcher who "did not throw good enough to hit." With Independence I swung at an awful lot of bad pitches, just from impatience and the knowledge that it was a long time between decent pitches. When I got where the pitchers could stay around the plate more, I began to connect better.

My spirits were good too. I was glad to be with Harry, and I guess glad to be still more or less in my own neighborhood. Joplin, after all, was just a short hop from Baxter Springs, where I had first started to make a name for myself, so there were fans of mine all through the area to yell for me when I stepped to bat. I responded by really tying into those big fat minor league fast balls.

With the whole season to work in, and no spells of homesickness to slow me down, with a manager who never bugged me, and a club once more that was winning nearly all its games, I set records at the plate. I had 199 hits, 27 home runs, 136 runs batted in and the biggest batting average of my pro career: .383. That was one of the merriest seasons I ever lived through. We played in bigger towns in this league: Fort Smith, Muskogee, St. Joe, and Hutchinson, where the hotels sometimes intimidated us a little. But the bus rides were wilder than ever it seemed. We just went on from cleaning up one series to cleaning up another, with hits rattling off every fence in the league. So we celebrated, roughhousing from one town to the next. Harry Craft, as usual, let his patience stretch to the very end. He had no desire, I guess, to utter a sound that might slow our momentum. Or perhaps he just figured that a club that won games at the rate we did was entitled to yank the whistle cord all day if we felt like it.

To an older player, I think, those Class C schedules could have been pretty rough, night games mostly, and long, hot bus rides, sometimes fairly primitive locker-room facilities and rock-hard playing surfaces. For a while the club had only six bats for the whole line-up. But it was a carnival to most of us, as long as those hits dropped in and those scores rolled up. Our season ended in mid-September, so the major league clubs could call up their option boys and work them out with the big team. The end of the season always meant celebrations and ceremonies, the very best of which, to me, was the day they announced the awards. I had been voted Most Valuable Player in the Western Association, and it tickled me to my bones to know my father was in the stands at Muskogee the night that announcement was made.

But, whether it was the added pressure or just more of

the same sort of chances I had been seeing all season, I made five fat errors that game, one easy straight-on ground ball going right through my legs to the outfield. I also fired the ball a few times five or six feet over the first baseman's head. After the fourth error I was in such a state of disgust with myself that I hardly knew what was going on around me. But somehow that runner was rubbed out and the next batter struck out. After the strike-out the ball was thrown around the infield and when it came to me, I just slapped at it, meaning to pick it off with a downward sweep of my glove, but really too burned up with myself to concentrate. The ball had been thrown hard and it skipped right through the fingertips of my glove and took me square on the mouth, knocking me back half a step and setting the blood to spurting inside my lips. That gave me twice as much reason to curse myself out. But instead it reminded me what a damn fool stunt it was to act this way, and I buckled down and played through the rest of the game with a nice fat lip that almost shut off my nostrils. I threw another ball into the stands too, but that one did not upset me.

My chief trouble on ground balls was that I never failed to flinch at the hard-hit ones, so that I would turn my face away and lift my chin when the ball was right upon me. A sudden change in bounce would take me unawares then, so that I could not adjust my glove to stop the ball. If I was lucky, I stopped it with my arm or chest or leg. If I was unlucky, it skittered on through my legs or caromed off my chin. All in all, I was a thorough-going butcher in the infield and I am sure every scout who ever saw me, as well as Harry Craft and any others who might have watched or managed me, reported emphatically that I was no shortstop. But I was doing more than holding my job with my bat. If I let in runs with my errors, I was belting them in twice over with long hits. And, except when I saw a good chance to drag a bunt, I was going for those long hits every time.

Casey Stengel decided when he first saw me (I learned afterwards) that I was never going to be a shortstop. But

I was not thinking much about the big leagues at that time. I was still a teen-ager, happy with a crowd mostly my own age, intensely satisfied with the way those baseballs were whistling off my bat, learning from Harry Craft more about how to be a baseball player and how to be an adult, and confident that when the time was ripe, I would get my chance with the club upstairs. Before that ever happened, I expected to play some double-A or even triple-A ball along with others on the Joplin roster. Big league ball looked to me the way college looks to a high-school sophomore.

But I was jumped right up to the big leagues just as soon as the season closed at Joplin—not to play in the majors, but just to travel with the Yankees and "get the feel" of belonging to the big team. By this time I had pretty well choked down the last of my homesickness and felt ready to go anywhere, in any company, without pangs. All the same, I was happy to discover that the Yankees had chosen another youngster, a hulking, good-natured, quiet type named Bill Skowron, to room with me on the trip and keep me company.

We were to stay with the Yankees throughout the western swing—to Detroit, Cleveland, Chicago, and St. Louis—working out before games, riding the bench, listening in at the strategy meetings. Neither Bill nor I was inclined to speak up when not spoken to, or butt into any conversations or any merry-making without an invitation. It was like a continual party anyway, to travel with the big club, suit up in major league parks, work out in front of major league fans, and aim some of our best shots at the fences in ball parks we had only read about. Bill was a city boy, born in Chicago, and had been playing his baseball at Purdue University, so I let him take the lead in almost everything we did, figuring he knew more about how to act in a big city than I did.

The only small fret I carried on this trip was a fear my money might run out. Hotel meals were costly, so Bill and I lived largely on hamburgers and milkshakes and a lot of french fries. Not a day went by on that trip that we did not attend at least one movie. I sometimes think of the bliss of those long September afternoons and evenings, and wonder if I could ever enjoy anything in life as much as I did those simple pleasures. Our young stomachs replete with cheap hot food (of a type that might floor me now) and satiated by a thick frosted, an ice cream and sticky sauce, with sometimes a bag of candy between us, we would wander among the strange lights and pick out the movie of our fancy. It never mattered if the show was good or bad. If it was good, we sat hypnotized to the end and then wandered out still under the spell. If it was bad, we laughed about it and repeated its worst parts to each other all the way home. But I honestly don't recall that there were so many bad ones. It seems to me that when you're that age, almost every movie is good. Some, of course, are better than others.

I got to see all the big team close up on this trip, but never felt that I knew them well. I was still too shy to approach any of them, particularly the ones like DiMaggio, who had always filled me with awe. Now, to sit right close to the great man as he stretched out his tired legs by his locker and called for a can of beer was something like having a seat near the President of the United States. I had no ambition to talk to him or even have him notice me (he did say "Hi kid!" sometimes), as long as I could gaze my fill at him when he was not looking.

Finally the team swung for St. Louis and the end of this particular idyll. I had spent pretty nearly every dime that I had held on to (after sending a good share of money home), but I did not in the least mind being broke. Just before the trip ended, Frank Scott, the road secretary, sent for me to meet him in his room. He sat there with a big checkbook before him and asked me briskly, "Now what have your expenses been on this trip? If you'll let me have the totals of your meal checks and so on, I'll give you your expense check."

I was honestly astounded, almost unable to speak. Expenses! When I spoke, it was just above a whisper. "Is the club going to *pay* me for the *meals* I ate?"

Frank laughed out loud. I must have been a picture of the country boy on his first trip away from home.

"Well, Mr. Weiss said I should be good to you," he said. "And we certainly expected to pay for your meals."

My God! All those hamburgers and french fries! Or rather, all those steaks that Bill and I passed up! Frank added up the days, multiplied them by some incredible sum of money—$10 or so, twice as much as I would have spent—and handed me a check. I had actually made a profit on the deal and I went home to Commerce so happy I could have made the whole distance in a series of jumps. So this is what it was like to be a Yankee!

I knew, of course, that I was not a Yankee yet. Bill Skowron was ticketed for Binghamton and I was already on the Binghamton roster for next season. But at the moment I had no thought but to get back to Commerce and tell Merlyn all the wonders of the cities I had seen, to go to football games, play ball with my father, and start to get ready for next spring. The Yankees surprised us all, however, by inviting the whole gang (I found out much later that this was a typical George Weiss gesture)—mother, father, twins, Merlyn, and me to the World Series in New York. That was a visit to paradise.

The next spring I went to Phoenix once more, feeling far more at ease this time, strong from an active winter, and ready to enjoy sending those baseballs streaking through that unresisting air. There was a collection of rookies there and one or two were far less at home than I was, so my own lonesomeness was somewhat reduced.

The men on the field, chiefly Bobby Brown and Jerry Coleman, who played on either side of me when I tried to be a shortstop, were endlessly helpful and patient. But after I had worked out in the infield one day, Casey came over to me and said mildly, "Ever think of playing the outfield?"

Then, as now, I was ready to play anywhere my manager asked me to and I was glad to have Tommy Henrich take me over to make me into an outfielder. There really is not too much to learn about that job as far as technique goes. If you can move fast and throw better than your grandmother, you can be an outfielder. I had done enough sprinting to be in the habit of running on my toes, as an outfielder must, and I could run fast enough to catch balls all over the landscape. Center field gives you plenty of room to roam, with hardly ever any need to make a sudden stop to keep from denting a fence.

Casey himself showed me a few of the fundamentals, which have mostly to do with using your brains to anticipate the play, so you will know what to do with the ball when you catch it. I learned to keep my throws low, so the cut-off man could get them as the throws crossed the diamond, and I learned to expect every ball to come my way. Catching fly balls and learning to judge them is nothing but practice. And I took plenty of that. Out on the green grass, in the embracing Arizona sun, or standing at the plate to take my cuts, I had no time to be lonely or even to think about anything more than playing baseball.

When we were not busy fielding or batting, there were always pepper games to keep the blood coursing and I enjoyed those, although I sometimes, in my enthusiasm, tapped the balls a little too hard when they were tossed up to me. One day, I will never forget, I rapped the ball extra sharply and it streaked right through the small group of rookie fielders, to bounce once and smack the leg of a player working out many yards away. That was Joe DiMaggio! The man I admired most of all the Yankees I had ever known and the one Yankee I probably stood most in awe of. I stood there open-mouthed and felt a tiny icicle of fear go down through my gut. I don't know what I expected Joe to do—turn and bawl me out, I suppose, or walk over and ask who the hell I thought I was and what I was doing there anyway.

But Joe just looked at me, darkly, but without anger, and went back to playing pepper. One of his mates picked up the ball and threw it back.

The Fates seemed determined to make Joe my special target, for some time later when we were playing a ball game and Casey called upon me to pinch-hit, Joe was sitting almost beside me on the bench. The summons to bat sent me jumping right to my feet. I yanked off my jacket in two quick moves, flung it behind me, and grabbed a bat from the rack. But there was a smothered yell from the bench and I turned, aghast to discover that I had tossed my jacket right in Joe's face and he was wearing it like a hood. I tried to gulp some sort of apology, but this time Joe laughed out loud. I turned my familiar purple in the neck, face, and ears and could still feel my cheeks burning when I stood at the plate.

Gradually I became more at home with the club, although I was a long way from feeling like a Yankee. But this time I knew I was learning major league ball and I ate up my lessons and put my whole heart in my practice.

Casey Stengel had me scared for a long time, for I had heard him snarl at some of the players and rasp out orders and advice like a testy schoolmaster. But he always treated me with patience, in a gentle voice, as if he had selected me as his special pet. He set me to practicing on fly balls that rebounded off the wall and if I ran too close and missed the rebound, he never bawled me out. Playing the outfield, I had plenty of chance to give my strong arm a workout, without any fear that the ball would go into the stands, and Casey seemed to enjoy seeing me throw. Most of all he enjoyed seeing me hit, and more than once he would give me a light swat on the rump as he came near me and told me I was a pretty good hitter.

There were many things about the game that I needed no coaching on. On the bases, Casey turned me loose, because he saw that I knew how to get a start on a pitcher and he had no fear that I would miss a chance. I didn't have to be taught how to catch a ball and while I more than once threw the ball to the wrong base after a catch, Casey corrected me in a kindly way and told me what was right and why. There must have been many young players as dumb as I was and probably a few even dumber, but I did all the same manage to pull some rocks that nobody else could match.

In one of our early exhibitions I played center field with Gene Woodling beside me in right. It was the first big league competition for me, for we were playing Cleveland and we were out to win. Early in the game I got my very first big league chance. Ray Boone hit a line drive straight at me. It was easy to line up and I moved in a few steps to take it chest high. The sun was bright and, in order to look professional in every way, I flipped my sunglasses down with a practiced finger. As soon as I did, the day went black! I was not looking into the sun and the ball disappeared completely. Before I could react to this phenomenon, the ball hit me square on the head, just above my nose, and bounced off as if it had struck a rock. I staggered for a second, pulled the glasses back, and looked foggily for the ball. It had bounded high, but not far, and Gene Woodling, ranging close, fielded it quickly and threw it in. Then he came back to me, and I tried to look suitably pained, apologetic, and bewildered. Actually, I did not have to try too hard, for the wallop had left me woozy and had raised a lump. And I was fiercely embarrassed. But Gene was not concerned with the state of my health or my soul.

"You break the glasses?" he demanded. I reached up numbly to examine them. "They're okay," I said. I wondered if I should tell him that *I* was not, but he just turned and trotted back to his position. I suppose he figured any kid dumb enough to blind himself that way must have a head hard enough to withstand a line drive.

But I did my share of good things too, mostly at the plate, and the approval of my new teammates came quickly and made my life easier. We worked our way gradually to New York, where we were to "open" with exhibition games against the Dodgers, then shove off to Washington to open the regular season in front of the President. Before the first game at the Stadium I came down early to the park—it is just a few blocks from the hotel where I stayed—and walked out on the grass to look up at the sweep of empty stands. Gee, it was big! There was not another place like it in the country just then. I tried to imagine it jammed with people, and me there at the plate driving a baseball out into those distant, dark seats. Well, that, I told myself, was still a year or two away. But I had no fault to find with my fate just then. I had stayed with the big club longer than I had expected. I was all over my homesickness and I felt strong and hopeful, ready for anything Casey Stengel might send my way.

Before we left New York, I had to fly back to Commerce to satisfy my draft board, and returned in time to play one game at Ebbets Field, where I learned that Casey had played in the dim past, right along those very walls where he now showed me how to watch for the angles and rebounds in right field. It was hard to think of him as once being young, like me, and trotting on this very grass in spikes, with no idea of the future.

The two or three other rookies who had been held over with the big team were slated to go to Binghamton now that the big league season was about to open. But the Yankees had another Class A club in Beaumont, Texas, and I knew that Harry Craft had been sent there. I was trying to get up nerve enough to tell Casey I would like to go to Beaumont too. But it was not until we were on the train to Washington that I found courage enough to ask Casey about this. I made a point of explaining that I wanted to be where Harry Craft was going to be. Casey squinted hard at me.

"How'd you like to stay with the Yankees?" he said.

The Yankees! How could that be? Jump from Class C to the *Yankees*? When I got my breath back, I made it plain to Casey that a miracle like that, if it could be worked, would put about an inch of frosting on my cake.

"All right," said Casey. "You come back here with me and meet Mr. Weiss. You let me do the talking. I'm going to see if I can get you a little more than the minimum."

The minimum then was $5,000 and that was more money than my father made. To get more than that meant that I could practically take over support of the family, or at least make things a whole lot easier for them . . . Or get married . . . Or . . . I could not begin to think of all the things I might be able to do with so much money in my pocket. In a sort of pink haze I trailed after Casey to the drawing room where George Weiss and Dan Topping sat in their shirt sleeves, looking wealthy, composed, and distant as the Rockies. Even if Casey had not told me to keep my mouth shut, I'd have been unable to speak. I shook hands with both of the big brass, then sat down to listen while Casey detailed all my virtues and explained why I had to have more than the minimum salary. There was no argument from Mr. Weiss. I nodded quick agreement to the figure they suggested. (I'd have taken half that, just to stay on with the big club.) The deal was made and I could feel myself beginning to grin all over. My first impulse when we got out of the drawing room was to run and telephone my father. But even if there had been a telephone on that train, I'd have not known how to use it or dared to try. So I sat down and savored my good luck all by myself in the Pullman chair, and I decided finally that the best way would be to wait until I had appeared in the line-up in Washington. Then I could send the clipping home, showing that Mickey Mantle had become a New York Yankee.

It rained all day, however, and there was no game in Washington, and before I could even write my father about it, he had learned through the newspapers that I had signed a Yankee contract.

The newspapers were nearly my undoing. They began to build me up as the successor to, if not actually the superior of, Joe DiMaggio! I was no more a Joe DiMaggio than I was a Bob Feller or a Babe Ruth. Someday, perhaps if I stayed in baseball long enough, I might begin to hit in Joe's class and work a few of the marvels he had worked, but now he was like the Washington Monument beside me. The writers, a breed I was just beginning to know, probably felt they were doing me favors by writing me up as if I were already ticketed to the

Hall of Fame. The result was that many of the home fans, whose love for DiMaggio passed even Joe's understanding, resented me right from the beginning, or resented my not delivering immediately on my newspaper promise. It may have been, too, that the fulsome write-ups had an insidious effect upon me, scaring me with the goals they set for me and giving me the notion that if I did not come through with new records at bat and in the field, I would be done for.

It took me a while to learn to be wary of writers. At first I thought you could talk to them just the way you might talk to any of the guys in the clubhouse—none of whom would think of running out and repeating some dumb thing you said, trying to make it sound dumber. It was a real shock to me to discover that when I said something in front of a writer, I was shouting it from the New York rooftops, and I began to avoid them when I could and keep my mouth shut when I could not. That, however, was a later development. In the beginning everything and everybody seemed wrapped in the same rosy cloud. I can remember when I first reached Washington, how I had to say it aloud to myself to realize that I was actually looking at the building they ran the country from, and not just seeing a picture on a postcard.

In New York I lived at the Concourse Plaza Hotel, which seemed to me the ultimate in luxury. I blush sometimes to think of what I must have looked like to them, with my cardboard suitcase that I had been so pleased with when it was shiny and new. (You could buy them for about $3.98 in the big-city drugstores, and I did not realize that they were any different from the best.) I had just one suit, my good suit, and saw no need for more. I never knew anyone at home, in my neighborhood, who had use for more than one good suit. For every day I had slacks and sports shirts and sweaters and I had one pair of shoes that did me for everything. Gradually, with the help of men like Hank Bauer, I came to understand that there was almost as much to learn about how to act off the diamond as there was about what to do when you were on. I found out what kind of shirts and neckties to buy; what to order for breakfast in a hotel and how big a tip to leave; where to get my hair cut; what some strange words on the menu meant; and how to avoid in a dozen ways making a fool of myself in public.

The fans were something else. I had never in my life played ball in front of so many thousands of people. But the size of the crowds did not really trouble me. The applause, like the roar of some animal, stirred me, of course, and the occasionally gathered boos irritated me a little. Usually when I did something to get booed for, such as a strike-out, I was a whole lot madder at myself than the crowd was and so hardly heard the noise. What did begin to pierce my hide, which was never exactly leathery, was the virulence of some of the insults that were tossed at me from the nearby stands. I well understood that my being made into a rival of Joe DiMaggio turned plenty of fans against me. But I was not ready for the dirty names or the screaming profanity or the tireless abuse. It scorched me for a while until finally I discovered a way to cope with it. When one voice, above all others, concentrated its venom on me, I would turn to the stands, locate the source of the noise, then look that fan right in the eye. It never failed to silence him. It was funny how the courage would go right out of a fellow when he found that not the mob, but he, in his lonesome self, was carrying on a personal quarrel with an athlete. It really wasn't meant to be personal at all, just part of the excitement.

Of course, in later years teen-agers seemed to grow wilder and to give real problems on occasion. But in the beginning they were not more than I could handle. I was a big leaguer now and would set out to act like one.

LESSON TWO

Like a good many baseball addicts, I played almost every position before I settled on the outfield. In the Pee Wee League I was a full-time catcher, with a "chest" protector that hit the ground in front of me when I squatted down. In high school I was a pitcher. But I never wanted that job, because in organized ball it meant you played only every fourth day.

Catching is probably the toughest job in the game and it is a worn-out joke that only numskulls would ever subject themselves to the punishment a catcher has to take. But catching takes the most brains and the most baseball knowledge, and many guys find it satisfying because the catcher practically runs the team on the field. He calls the pitches, watches the base-runners, keeps the infielders on their toes, moves the outfielders, and helps the manager decide when a pitcher must come out. He also acts as captain on infield pop-flies, deciding which man shall take the ball. And of course he has to scramble after bunts.

The Yankees always had strong catching, chiefly, I think, because they have had good instruction from Bill Dickey, Ralph Houk, and Jim Hegan. Bill practically made Yogi Berra into a catcher, by hand. And Ralph and Jim have brought our young catchers along so fast that we always seem to have one ready to move in. Yogi, of course, was in a class by himself, once he learned to get out of the chute and get those throws off hard and fast. But Elston Howard, besides being one of my favorite people, is one of the greatest catchers alive. I may be wrong about this, but I think Ellie has never in all his career missed a pop-foul—and has never suffered a broken finger. So he may be the best man to use for a model.

One thing you will notice about Ellie is that he plays right up close behind the bat, just as close as he can get without danger of being hit by the bat. He adjusts his position to each batter, moving up closer when the batter stands forward in the box, and giving a little ground when he is dealing with one of those guys who stands far back in the batter's box. Ellie says that this gives him a better jump on a foul. He sees it quicker and I think can tell too from the sound of it if he is going to have a play. One thing I observed was that Ellie hardly ever goes back after a foul that he has no play on. He just seems able to tell immediately how high and far the ball is going. When he does go after a foul, he takes off his mask and holds on to it until he sees where the ball is, then he throws the mask away from the ball. In catching the ball, he gets it right over his head, so that it is coming straight down at him, and takes it in both hands, with the glove at eye level. As I said, he never misses. At least I have never seen him miss, and I hope I am not jinxing him by saying this.

What holds some catchers back, I think, is that they are afraid to throw. They are so afraid of making a bad throw that they hold the ball until they have an almost sure play. But the really great catchers—Roy Campanella, for instance—would throw every time they caught the runner leaning the wrong way. They were always ready to step out of their position toward first or third and rifle the ball down, either to hold a runner close or to catch him with too big a lead. Roy really was a menace to a base-runner. He was fast and aggressive and he would never allow a base-runner to hold a big lead or to "lean" toward second base after a pitch. Ellie is the same way and Yogi too learned to have confidence in his ability to hit the target with a quick throw any time. The target, at second, is the bag. The throw should get there about knee high.

Of course, a catcher's main job is to catch the ball—to keep it from going through to the backstop. To be certain about this, he uses his body as well as his hands. The next time you see the Yankees in action, just watch Ellie or young Jake Gibbs on an outside pitch, or a pitch in the dirt. They will not reach after the ball with one hand. They will either slide over to get the whole body in front of the ball or drop to their knees and keep the ball from bouncing through.

Our catching coach, Jim Hegan, disagrees with Ellie on one thing. Jim likes to use the old-fashioned glove with no break in the rim, while Ellie favors the one you can fold over like a fielder's glove. Jim says that with the new type glove you have a tendency to slap down on a low pitch and actually knock it out of the strike zone as you glove it, while the solid-rim glove forces you to hold the pitch up and make it less likely the umpire will misjudge it. I guess it's a matter of what you are comfortable with. Ellie's work does not seem to suffer from using that glove—even though, like every catcher, he had just as soon not have to cope with a knuckle-baller. Those fellows really drive a catcher to distraction, because even *they* don't know just where the ball is going. Ellie tried an oversize glove, when the Yankees had Bob Tiefenauer for a while, but the glove was so stiff and unyielding that Ellie could not hang on to the ball, and he had several passed balls—something Ellie just despises to be guilty of. Finally he discovered that it was better to use his regular glove and just to *snatch* at the ball at the last second. But I think he was secretly delighted when knuckle-balling Bob was traded off.

Generally, to be a catcher, I think you need to be long-armed and agile, so you can jump out fast either to field a bunt or throw to a base or to get down to back up the first baseman. Good size helps, especially in blocking the plate against a sliding runner. But if you just remember to hold the ball in *both* hands and hold it tight, you can usually make put-outs at the plate without necessarily stopping the runner cold. My trouble as a catcher was the same as my trouble as an infielder—wild throws. A catcher needs to practice long and hard throwing at a target. He does not wind up to throw, because he hasn't time. He has to cock his arm and snap that throw right off. But he should step forward toward the base when he fires the ball and really get his back into it. You can't afford to steer the ball from that position. You have to fire it out of a cannon. Maybe when you first begin, you'll be heaving the ball into center field. But let it go. Eventually, you'll correct your aim and zero in. Just don't get timid about throwing.

I think if I had not been able to hit the way I did, I'd have preferred pitching, because a pitcher is in command of the baseball and probably gets more kicks out of the game than any other single player. I was like a lot of kids when I began—thinking more of trick pitches than of control. Actually no trick pitch is ever as effective in getting batters out as a good hard fast ball. That will always be the prime pitch in any league. And if you can keep the ball low, you can be pretty sure no one will hit it too far. There have not been too many players who could drive a low pitch for distance. Al Rosen was one, but offhand I cannot think of others. So if you aim to do any pitching, you should work first of all on learning to keep the ball low. A youngster who wants to be a pitcher should do plenty of throwing, and should always throw at targets. Some great pitchers, they say, learned their trade by throwing rocks when they were kids. Bob Turley says he got his start throwing pears in his back yard in St. Louis. But you can always find something to throw and something to throw at. Eventually you will want to have a catcher to throw to, then you should work—before you do anything else—on keeping that ball below his waist. You can't call yourself a pitcher until you get this kind of control. And when you have that ability to keep the ball low, you can start trying to keep it over the plate. You'll find that will be relatively easy, once you have your up-and-down control.

Of course, you need something besides a fast ball, because the real secret of pitching is to keep the batter off balance. A curve ball is easy to learn and no matter what anyone says, it does not hurt anybody's arm to start throwing curves, even at an early age. Most people who know about such things will advise kids not to throw knuckle balls when they are young and strong. But that is just because a knuckle ball, because it requires no strength, will not help your arm develop. You need lots of throwing—with the full strength and the full length of your arm—to grow into a pitcher. Throwing from the elbow, or with the arm pulled in, just will not give you the workout you need.

A curve is thrown off the edge of the fingers instead of off the fingertips. That is, the hand is turned sharply, as you deliver the ball, so the palm is up and the ball rolls out of the gap between thumb and forefinger. This gives the ball that peculiar spin that causes it to dip down and away from the batter. (A right-hander's curve will break away from a right-handed batter, and a lefty's curve will break away from a lefty. Of course, a switch-hitter never has the curve breaking away from him.) But before you try to control the curve, you have to control the fast ball. In amateur ball you'll go a long way on a good fast ball and good control. And in between times you can practice your curve when you are ahead of the batter.

I never did get to see much of the really great fast-ballers in action. But when Bob Turley was right, I don't believe I ever saw anyone throw a ball any harder. Bob had a pretty good curve too, but he used that mostly as his waste pitch, just to let the batter know that there was another pitch that was likely to come, at a different speed. When Bob's fast ball was not blazing, however, he was not nearly so effective. Once Casey lifted Bob from a ball game when he had a lead and Bob had not yet gone far enough to get credit for the win. Bob really was sizzling with anger and could not see why he had to come out. Casey's explanation was that Bob had not been striking out enough batters. It was a fact that if Bob did not fan one out of every three or four men to face him, you could be sure his fast ball was not smoking as it should. After he calmed down, Bob had to admit Casey was right.

There is an awful lot more to pitching than I could begin to explain in a book like this. But believe me, if you have a good fast ball and a good curve and can keep both of them low and over the plate, you need nothing else. Sliders and sinkers are most effective, but you can go a long way without them. They make good extra pitches, which you can work on after you have established yourself.

But one thing you will find out if you go in for pitching is that it puts great demands on your legs. Pitchers need to run, every single day, distance runs and wind-sprints both, to build up their stamina. You cannot neglect that, or you'll not stay in fast company very long. Even today I see Hank Bauer running the legs off his pitchers before a game begins—sprint, sprint, sprint, until that old sweat really pours off.

I don't know if off-the-diamond behavior is of first importance to a ballplayer, but it seems to me that it is bound to have some effect on a man's career. Most of the really great stars I have known have carried themselves with a certain amount of dignity in public. Of course I have read, as everybody else has, of the rambunctious heroes of years ago who used to take over a hotel or even a city block, and carry on as if it were their private playground. When you are a kid, you are bound to cut up some if you are away from all restraint. But I still think that it pays to cultivate self-respect, to avoid slopping around in public as if you had just rolled out of bed, to stay shaven and clean and pulled together, and to comport yourself with some regard for the feelings of the people near you.

I can still see, in my mind's eye, rugged Harry Craft walking down the street, well set up, neatly dressed, looking like a man of the sort you do not bump into at every corner. And I know that this posture of his made a deep impression on his charges, made it easier for him to maintain control, and made us all ready to accept him as a leader. I do not mean that he swaggered or appeared impressed with his own importance. Quite the opposite. He was always quiet and unassuming in manner, and he never looked as if he were trying to make a show of himself. But he stood up straight and looked the whole world in the eye. And his appearance was always neat, brushed, and polished.

Having a good time, going to parties, staying up late—these have nothing to do with what I am talking about. I am not the man to give lectures on the value of abstemious behavior. My subject is self-respect. I have known several professional athletes, even with the Yankees, who devoted a lot of time to clowning, who dressed sloppily, gagged it up around hotel lobbies, made a point of never taking anything seriously, and cavorted in a manner so silly sometimes that it was almost unbalanced. And it never failed that these were the men who wound up being traded from one club to another and finally faded right out of the game.

When you make baseball your profession, you have to be serious about it. You have to practice seriously, because the habits you form in practice are the habits you will carry into the game. And in the game itself you have to keep bearing down. This does not mean that you cannot enjoy the game. On the contrary, you actually enjoy it more if you put your whole heart into it. You do that when you realize that the game demands your best, that you cannot play it with one hand behind you and one eye on the stands, that to advance in our profession you must make every game, every inning, every play a full-time job. I read recently that one reason Jim Bunning is such a tough pitcher to hit is that he "throws every pitch as if it was the final pitch in the World Series." That's what I mean by taking the game seriously. If you think of yourself as a clown or a "character," you cannot have the self-respect required to take your profession seriously.

Of course, I believe in relaxing when the game is over. I even believe in cutting up a little and in sharing laughs in the clubhouse or the hotel or a night club. But I'm opposed to playing for laughs, either on the field or off. And I'm against sloppiness.

Sometimes, of course, play can look sloppy when it is really just inexpert. Lord knows I used to try hard enough on those ground balls. It is just that I never could break that habit of flinching, of lifting my face to get it out of the way of the ball. And then I was always in too much of a rush to get my throws off.

To field a ground ball properly, you have to get your head right over it. You must get close to the ground, by bending your knees and bending your back. Just squatting with a straight back, like a jack-in-the-box, is no way to field a ball, for it does not allow you to sight the ball sharply. And trying to bend over without bending your knees puts you off balance and makes it hard for you to reach the ball.

Ideally, you field the ball out in front of you. Your feet, if you are charging the ball as you should, will be separated in a normal stride, one ahead of the other. The glove should reach out—further out than your front foot—to smother the ball. And to be successful at this you have to have more courage than I had about getting your head down. Casey Stengel used to teach us that an infielder should bend down until he could sight the underside of his cap-bill in front of him. Actually, if you get down like that and keep your eye on the ball, there is very little chance it will hit you, for you will react automatically to the bounce.

You must charge every ground ball. The sooner you get to it, the more time you will have to make the play, and the better your chance will be of nailing the runner. Of course, there will be occasionally rocket-speed balls that get to you almost before you can move, and on these you may even have to drop back a half-step. But you will be ready for these if you maintain an aggressive, go-get-'em attitude toward ground balls.

You will find, as I did, that the balls you can get an angle on, the ones you can approach from one side of their line of flight, will be the easiest to judge. So the ones you need to practice on most will be the balls coming straight at you. It is far more difficult on such balls to judge the bounce and the speed, and on these the temptation is always greater to let the ball play you, rather than vice versa. That is, you may find yourself backing off, or adjusting your stance to conform with the expected bounce, instead of reaching out and smothering the ball. So when you take infield practice, try to get a lot of those straight-at-you balls, hit hard enough to give you a real problem.

If you watch amateur baseball a lot, you will notice that most kids miss ground balls by not getting their hands down low enough. That is, the balls will get by because they skip *under* the glove. But when pros make errors, the balls most often go over the glove, run up the arm, or bounce off the body. That is because the pros have learned to *dig* those ground balls out, even if it means scraping dirt. Many times you will see a big league infielder come up from fielding a ball with the dirt running out between the fingers of his glove.

My throws were off target every now and then because I

would fail to take the time to make them good. On most really hard-hit balls, unless you have to go a long way after them, you will have time enough to straighten up, sight your target clearly, and gun the ball to the base with an overhand throw. The speed of the throw will more than make up for the extra half-second you require. But you should always look at the target and make sure there *is* a target. Sometimes there may be nobody covering the base. It is up to you to make sure and not fire the ball at the opposition coach or the umpire.

I was better on double-play throws than on the throws to first, because these did not take any strength and I was not tempted to use my full power. On a toss to second, to start a double play, or to catch a runner coming down, take care to time your toss so it reaches the other fielder when he is a stride or two off the base. If you hold the ball until the fielder is on the base, he may be off the base when he takes the throw and the man may be safe. So get it to him a step or two ahead of time. To start a double play, give the ball to your partner about chest high, so his hands will be in throwing position. And never flip the ball to him from behind your glove. Sometimes, of course, you may have to make the toss with the gloved hand if the play is close. Then be sure you turn the glove so he can see the ball. On a toss with the throwing hand, be sure you clear your glove out of there. Pull your left arm away, so the glove will not shut off your partner's view of the ball. Face him squarely as you throw and move toward the base.

The Yankees had some great double-play combinations during my time and they used to work together as if they were operated by the same machine. I don't believe there was ever a greater shortstop, when he was at his best, than Phil Rizzuto. I never saw anyone range farther than he did, or get throws off faster. On a double play, working with Jerry Coleman, he was a magician. If the ball came to Coleman, Phil would be scooting for the bag almost before the ball had taken its first bounce, slowing himself sometimes with little pitty-pat steps, so he could take that throw as he approached the base. Jerry would feed it to him with a quick twist of his body and a hard snap throw, so the ball would reach Phil about chest high. Then Phil would scamper across the base, dragging one foot over it to make the tag, and fire the ball down without a wasted motion. Sometimes the runner would be right on top of him and Phil would go up into the air like an acrobat, both knees bent to keep his shins out of the way, facing the first baseman squarely, and snapping off that overhand throw from right behind his ear.

Bobby Richardson was a great man to watch at second base. There was no one better at twist and throw, where the fielder, having no time to shift his feet, just twists hard to the right, so that his right knee hits the dirt, to zip the ball to the pivot man in a split second.

If you are the pivot man on the play, there are many different ways to handle the double plays and I don't intend to go into all of them. I never learned them all anyway. The safe way to do it and probably the best for beginners is to hit the base with one foot then back off to make your throw to first. In this way you can avoid the runner's effort to throw you off balance. But one thing you have to be sure about: Square around and face first base directly before you throw. Don't take chances on uncorking an off-balance, out-of-the-ball-park heave, the sort I used to specialize in.

When you tag a runner out at second base, you cannot be chicken about it. If you make the tag close to the base, and get your head right over the ball, you can get the ball on the runner and get out of there safely. Don't try to tag a sliding runner up on the body somewhere. Get the ball down in front of his target—the base. Don't get it down too soon and invite him to kick it away. Sweep it down there as he starts his slide and get it out of there when the tag is made. Some ballplayers get cut on this play because they turn the gloved hand palm out to make the tag. Remember, you don't have to get the ball on him. If you get the glove that holds the ball on him, he's out. So turn your hand around to present the back of your wrist to the runner. The inside of your wrist is far more susceptible to cuts than the back is. Not that you really get scratched so often. But now and then you may not move your hand with the usual deftness, so you might as well play safe.

Frank Crosetti once showed me all the scars he carries on the inner side of his left wrist, from getting cut while trying to tag runners out. It took Cro a long time to learn to turn his hand around and present the back of it to the runner. You might as well learn it without the scars.

One big advantage I had while with the Yankees was having such good teachers around me—not only Cro, but men like Tommy Henrich, Gene Woodling, and Joe DiMaggio. Joe of course was one of the greatest center fielders who ever lived and only people who never saw him in action would imagine that I could move in and take his place. He used to glide over that turf like a skater on smooth ice and make easy catches out of balls that might have gone yards beyond any other fielder. The secret was that Joe got a great jump on a ball, and was usually started for it a split second after it left the bat. I think Joe could get a line on a ball by the sound it made on the bat and would know immediately whether he would have to move in or start back. As a result, he would be moving back, graceful and smooth as a dancer, with his eye fixed on the ball, and take it right over his shoulder as if it were a bird coming to nest. His throws were almost geometrically perfect, never too high for the cut-off man, never more than a foot or two off target.

Some outfielders play a stationary field, moving only when they sight the ball. But big Joe was always drifting right or left, deep or shallow, depending on the hitter, the score, and the tactical situation. For instance, with a man on second base and nobody out, Joe would often smell a hit to right field and he would begin to drift that way almost before the pitcher let go of the ball. Then, if the batter did happen to get the ball too high, Joe would be right there to nail it, and it would take a mighty rash base-runner to try to go to third after the catch.

Outfielding, as I said, is a whole lot easier to learn than playing the infield. Most good runners do not need to be told to run on their toes, because that is the natural way to go when you try to get up some speed. Running on your heels jars your spine and makes your vision blur so it is very difficult to judge the flight of a ball accurately.

It probably takes an extra lot of practice pursuing fungo

flies to learn to judge the balls that come straight at you. The one that is going to take off and go over your head and the one that is going to drop suddenly far in front of you—these do not look much different when they leave the bat. At the Yankee Stadium, the view from center field is not quite what you might imagine. The rise of the pitcher's mound cuts off the batter from the knees down and the ball sometimes seems to come up out of the ground. The haze of cigarette smoke that a big crowd can create and the sharp shadows that the late sun throws make it hard to pick up a view of the ball quickly too. I think, however, that practice helps you judge a ball by the sound made when the bat strikes it, and the speed at which it approaches gives it a different appearance too.

But all you need, to learn how to position yourself so you can handle these balls, is practice. You won't get all you need of that in a ball game, so you have to have someone to hit fungoes to you by the hour. You should always make yourself familiar with the ground you are playing on too, and take a view of the sun so you'll know what sort of fly is likely to give you trouble and require sunglasses. After my experience with stopping a line drive with my skull, Tommy Henrich showed me how to play a ball in the sun. The best way is to try first to pick it up out of the corner of your eye, taking a turn away from it to get a sideways slant on it. This keeps the sun from hitting you full in the eye and blinding you, and often when you get a slant on the ball like this, you can run it down without ever having to sight directly into the glare. In any event, you never give up on it, even when it is out of sight. It may come back into view at the last second and allow you to grab it.

Playing the fences takes some practice too, because fences vary from park to park. In big league parks, the warning track lets you know when you are getting close to the fence. But if you think you have a chance to glove the ball, even against the fence, you go right after it. If you know the ball is going to get to the fence ahead of you, you have to put on the brakes and keep from crowding the ball too close. Out in old Ebbets Field, where Casey gave me my first lessons, the fences were concrete, and a ball that struck those used to take off as if it had been hit again. You had to stay a lot further away from them than you would if the fence had been boards. A ball that streaks to the fence on the ground is going to bound off at the same angle it approached the fence, but in the other direction, so you have to allow for this as you run the ball down. Henrich was a great man at playing that tricky fence in right field at Yankee Stadium, and he nailed many a runner who was trying for an extra base on a ball that rebounded.

An outfielder expects every ball to come his way, and he tells himself in advance of every play just what he is going to do with the ball when he gets it. If he catches it on the fly, will he have a throw home? Or will there be a runner going from second to third? I know a lot of kids with good arms like to throw home at every chance, even when there is no hope at all of catching the runner. But sometimes you can choke a rally off by throwing to second base to get the man who hit the ball. Many times he will take for granted that you will try to cut off the run and he may come coasting in to second for an easy out.

They say the sign of a poor outfielder is throwing behind the runner. Players do that when they have not figured out ahead of time where the runner is and where to throw. But I found sometimes that I could rifle a ball in and catch a runner from behind when he was taking a routine turn at either first or second. You can get away with this when the runner has already given up hope of making that extra base and is just making the turn to be ready in case of an overthrow, or when a slow runner is trying to advance and has made up his mind the throw is going to some other base. It is a chancy play and you need a good strong arm and fast reflexes to get away with it. But when it works, it can demoralize the opposition.

Even when you throw to the plate, you have got to keep that throw down where the cut-off man can grab it. The ball should come in about head high over the diamond. Those humpbacked high-arc throws are another sign of poor outfielding. If your arm is not strong enough to sizzle the ball in on a trolley line, then you should throw to a relay man, who will run out part way to meet the throw. The relay man, an infielder, is bound to have a strong, accurate arm and if he keeps one eye on the base-runners, as he should, he will know just what to do with the ball when he gets it.

You see some relay men, even in the big leagues, who will run out to get a throw, with their backs turned to the infield. This is wrong. The relay man has to keep an eye on the runner while waiting for the throw. He does not need to face the outfielder squarely in order to catch the throw, but can stand with his body angled slightly toward the infield, so the runner will never be out of his sight. Of course, he will be waving his arms over his head so you can spot him immediately.

Outfielders have to help each other out. Gene Woodling was able to field the ball that bounced off my skull, because he automatically moved close to be right there if I needed help. You should know the abilities of your two outfield mates so you can judge whether to extend your own range to take fly balls that might be theirs, or whether to let them poach on your territory. And you should always tell each other what you are doing. If you get a good jump on a ball that is a bit out of your territory, you have to yell, "I've got it!" loud enough and often enough so the other fellow will not try for it. Or if he wants a ball that you might reach, you can tell him, "Take it!" Just be sure you don't wind up bowing each other into the play, so that nobody takes the ball at all.

If you ever had the idea that big leaguers don't occasionally foul up on simple plays of this sort, you should try to get a picture sometime of the 1961 World Series, the one where I spent most of my time on the bench. In the third game, in the seventh inning, with Tony Kubek on second base, I contributed a strike-out. But then Yogi lifted a soft fly to short right field. Elio Chacon, the rookie from Venezuela, went for it like a streak. But Frank Robinson, who was in right field that day, also came charging in at top speed, hoping to pick the ball off his shoe-tops. He grabbed it too, for he can really move over the grass. But little Elio had never slowed down, and he banged right into Robbie with a thud that made the earth tremble. Next thing you know, there were those two Cincinnati players stretched out cold on the grass, while Kubek galloped home. After that I am sure Elio remembered to call for the ball when he felt he had it.

This is all pretty elementary stuff and most people pick up this knowledge in school. But this just goes to show how simple a job outfielding is anyway. There is almost nothing to learn that a boy cannot get hold of with some steady practice. I don't believe in giving lessons in catching fly balls, either with thumbs up or down, or hands held high or low. I have seen fly balls caught in all sorts of ways. Just do it in the way it comes easiest to you and I guarantee they'll call the man out.

The main thing is not to forget the men on base. This is just a matter of staying alive, alert, and in the ball game. If there is a man on third base who will try to score—and if you really have a chance to get him—it is often a good idea to try to time your catch so you will be moving toward the diamond when you take the ball. This will give your throw added momentum, because you will be able to make it while you are moving in. Sometimes, when there is a man on third, it may be worth while to let a long foul fly drop, rather than catch it for the out and see the run score. And when you have the winning run on third in the ninth inning with the home club at bat, you will have to play in close, to catch the short drives. In that situation, a long fly is going to win the ball game whether it is caught or not.

chapter three

It seemed to me that my big league career was a mighty brief one, for it was all over (I thought) in a matter of weeks. I was doing reasonably well at the plate and had managed to handle nearly everything that came my way in the outfield, with only one or two real dumb mistakes. Then the club went to Boston and a long lean right-hander named Masterson struck me out five times. Each time I faced him I seemed to get worse. I would get one high, inside fast ball after another, the kind any strong batter ought to be able to drive out of the park, and I would miss the ball each time by what seemed to me at least twelve inches. I was always going for the distance anyway, unless I was bunting, so I really stirred that Boston air, until it must have ruffled the feathers of the harbor gulls. I had not been so handcuffed, or so humiliated, since I started taking money for playing ball. I knew a lot of curse words by that time and I applied them all, out loud, to myself, as I returned each time to the bench and, once under cover, I took a kick at the water cooler. If someone had showed me a baseball right then, I believe I'd have grabbed up my bat and knocked it right out of his hand, and probably have torn his hand off with it.

In the locker room I never spoke to anyone anyway, because I was simply too bashful to start a conversation. The man next to me was Joe DiMaggio, and he overawed me so that it would be a long time before I could do more than exchange a hello with him. So mostly I brooded in silence on what Masterson had done to me. Then it came to me that there had been another lanky pitcher in my past who had done the same. Long John Blair, in the Gabby Street League, had made a public idiot of me several times, and I had eventually cured him by dragging bunts. I made up my mind that next time I would do exactly the same. I was as fast as anyone I had met in the majors and I knew that if I could not hit a pitcher, I could surely outrun him.

This thought provided me comfort enough so that my spirits had lifted by the time we reached Detroit. In *this* game, I promised myself, I would get on base if I had to break an ankle trying.

Before the game began, Casey called me to his cubbyhole, to give me some advice, I imagined, about dealing with high, inside pitches. I was all ready to explain what I would do next time. But next time, I suddenly learned, was not coming. In a perfectly gentle way, but with complete bluntness, Casey told me I was being sent to Kansas City. I don't believe he quite realized what he was doing to me. He gave me the usual assurances that I would be back up, but I took this for no more than a crude effort to take the curse off the sentence he had just passed.

I went blindly and wordlessly back to the hotel and started at once for Minneapolis, where the Kansas City club was playing. Casey probably assumed that, as I had been ready to go to Beaumont, in double-A ball, it would be no serious jolt to find myself in Kansas City, which was triple-A then. But he might as well have told me he was shipping me back to Independence. I had been a Yankee, and now I was nothing. I was always one of those guys who took all bad luck doubly hard, who saw disaster when there was just everyday trouble, and who took every slump as if it were a downhill slide to oblivion. The trip to Minneapolis was mercifully short, but I remember none of it. I was too choked up to tell anyone good-bye and too blind with misery to take any note of passing scenery.

With Kansas City I had a momentary resurgence of hope when I told myself that I would make a quick comeback by dragging a bunt safely, and showing Casey and everybody else that I *could* get on base any time I wanted. So in my very first time at bat, against a right-hander, I picked out a good pitch, ran to meet it and put it neatly down where the pitcher could not reach it. I made first base with a yard to spare and stood there trying to look properly blasé, but feeling almost good enough to smile again. When the inning was over, I trotted modestly in to the bench to pick up my glove, and manager George Selkirk gave me a sour look that startled me.

"They didn't send you down here to bunt!" he growled. "They sent you down here to hit."

That finished me. I felt like the little boy who brought home a mud pie for a present and got himself a licking. As I went out to my position, I could feel the tears of self-pity stinging my eyes. What did a guy have to do? I asked myself.

What I did was go to bat twenty-two times in a row without a hit. Whatever I had had, I told myself, I had lost it now and my baseball career was over. It had all been too good too soon anyway, and I had no more heart for the big leagues or even for triple-A. I would go back home, take my job in the mines, play ball for money in the summer, and save up to marry Merlyn. I knew my father would sympathize with me, for he had had his own disappointments in baseball. I really longed to have him beside me, to put his arm over my shoulder and tell me that it was all right, that I had tried and failed, and that everybody was looking forward to having me home again. For a time I had been ashamed to write him of my disgrace, but now I asked him to come meet me in Kansas City and take me home. Home. That word never sounded so full of comfort before.

When my father met me in Kansas City, I could not speak for crying. My throat was squeezed tight and tears ran down my cheeks. But my father's eyes were ablaze. He started in on me without preliminaries:

"If that's the way you're going to take this," he said, "you don't belong in baseball anyway. If you have no more guts than that, just forget about the game completely. Come back and work in the mines, like me."

His tone, as much as his words, went right down through me and froze my toes. There was not a trace of sympathy in his eye. I had been looking for a comforting pat on the back and I had not even gotten a handshake. Get back on the field and play ball, he told me, if you've got the guts for it, and if not, then make up your mind right now you're through with the game for good.

I wanted to tell him that I *had* tried, that I had been up at bat twenty-three times with only a bunt single to show for it. But I knew better than to argue with my father when he was in this mood. I just had to bite back my shock and surprise and tell him I wanted to stay and try to do what he wanted me to do.

I did too. With his words still searing the underside of my soul, I went to bat that night and hit two home runs and I felt so damn good about it I nearly broke into tears anyway. And that night I got the handshake and the pat on the back that I had longed for. And I began to suspect that I had grown into a man.

That, I think, was the greatest thing my father ever did for me. All the encouragement he had given me when I was small, all the sacrifices he had made so I could play ball when other boys were working in the mines, all the painstaking instruction he had provided—all these would have been thrown away if he had not been there that night to put the iron into my spine when it was needed most.

I played in about 35 more games for Kansas City that year and had 121 more at bats. In that time I got 57 more hits, including 9 home runs, 3 triples, and 9 doubles. Altogether I knocked in 50 runs and ran my batting average up to .360 before Stengel decided I had perhaps learned a little about my strike zone and sent for me to come back to the big team.

This time I knew I was going to stay, and I knew there was big money just ahead—money that would make it possible for the Mantle family to live in comfort without worry and backbreaking labor, money that would enable Merlyn and me to get married. I began to come out of my shell more as my confidence grew, but I was still too bashful to speak to Joe DiMaggio, unless he spoke to me first. And I was still too much of the country boy to share all the excitement of big city life and act at home in a big hotel or a fancy restaurant. I had still not even gotten used to the hair-raising expense of taking a taxi ride in this city. Why it would cost you more than two dollars to get downtown!

I got one extra good break at this time. Frank Scott, who had been our traveling secretary and was now getting into business for himself as a ballplayers' agent, went away for the summer and left his apartment to Hank Bauer and Johnny Hopp. They asked me to share the place with them. It was right down in the White Light district, upstairs over the Stage Delicatessen, and it could not have been more happily situated for me, nor could I possibly have had a better sponsor, companion, and adviser than Hank turned out to be. Hank actually raised me the way no father could have, for he was a companion, sharing my tastes and my leisure, as well as a sympathetic friend who could give me the sort of intimate advice that you would never think to ask for—like what was wrong with my taste in clothes, why I shouldn't forget to tip a cabbie, and how to dodge some of the corny hazing they used to go in for in the clubhouse—the calls from Mr. Lyon and Mr. Fish (at the zoo and the aquarium, of course) and the adoring admirers that didn't exist.

The handiness of the Stage Delicatessen made my life easier in many ways. Like all shy people I had a hard time going into new restaurants, not knowing whether to grab a table or wait to be shown, afraid to order something different for fear of making a jerk of myself, unable sometimes to tell the waiter from the busboy. But in the Stage Delicatessen I might have been in my home town. Max and Hymie Asnas, who owned the place, became my good friends, made me feel welcome any time of day or night, and urged me to order anything I might happen to prefer, whether it was listed or not.

I also managed to brush the edges of what seemed to me the real Night Life of New York. The Stage was naturally a place where stage people collected after the show and I sat near enough to many of the famous Broadway names of the day to feel, for a few moments anyway, that I was one of them. That sort of stuff meant a lot more to me then than it ever did later, for I was still, at heart, a tourist, even if I was collecting a little fame of my own. And it still gave me a thrill to see in the flesh the men and women whose names decorated the gossip columns. As for myself, I was a hero to Max and Hymie at least. They provided me a handy haven where I could take all my meals in good friendly company, and a hangout that was far more fun and far healthier too than some corner tavern. Then there was Hank Bauer to help me choose my ties and shirts and explain to me the need of an extra suit of clothes and to advise me to get rid of my jay-bird suitcase and get one that befitted a successful young baseball player. It was all in all a fine summer, full of good times and good friends, right down where you could feel (or thought you could feel) the heart of the great city beating.

Of course I did not have half the money that some of my companions had. My salary looked big to me, however, particularly when we were on the road, with the club picking up the meal tabs. As families dependent upon the mine went, my family had always been comfortable, and my father was never tight-fisted. But if I needed an extra dollar or two, I had to work for them, and many things I thought I might like I had to do without. Often I had to do a good deal of scrounging and scratching to finance a date, or pass up parties for lack of wheels and lack of money. I get the impression nowadays that teen-agers have all the money in the world, and never have to squirm in their seats and dig casually into their pockets to sneak a surreptitious look at the roll before giving an order in a restaurant.

Anyway, I can say I was in shape to appreciate money when it came my way. It was small potatoes really, and not much more than what would be the minimum salary nowadays. But it was pure gravy to me, or at least it was until Hank began to smarten me up on the need to dress a little less like Johnny-in-the-Texas-League. It took me a while to adjust to the idea that a sports jacket that might have caused my high-school chums to snicker was really stylish and slick, and that shoes that might have knocked out a girl's eyes in Muskogee were strictly from the wheat belt in New York. I had a hard time too getting away from the hamburgers and malteds of my boyhood, to savor steaks such as only rich men were supposed to eat, to dare to order "a la carte" after an apprenticeship to club breakfasts. But once I'd made the change, I adjusted quickly, with Hank always there to keep me from saying or doing something extra stupid, such as trying to pay for a shoeshine that was going to go on the barbershop check, or trying to keep my new topcoat with me in a fancy restaurant.

Does sudden easy money spoil a youngster? Maybe it does. I would not grant, however, that my money was really easy, after what I had gone through emotionally to get it. And I don't feel that the good living and the good times and the good clothes spoiled me at all. I liked them and I still do and I would not begrudge them to anyone. It seems to me that a guy who spends money to have a good time really understands the value of money, just as long as he does not throw it away or deprive members of his family of things they need. I have run into a lot of men, in baseball and out, who guard their pennies as if they were all going to be cut off at the source tomorrow, who save on their meal money, do without decent clothes, chisel on tips—and insist that people who spend freely "don't know the value of a dollar." But it strikes me that any kid who has been hard up and had to struggle to get the good things of life knows more about what a dollar will do than anyone who is afraid to spend it.

I soon enough had reason to be thankful that there was extra money available, to pay doctors' bills. I would have spent the last I had if it would have done any good. But right at the moment I had no notion of what disasters lay ahead. I came back to the Yankees with much more confidence in my ability at the plate and hit thirteen home runs in what was left of the season. But I still struck out often and still became enraged at myself when I did so. These temper fits were not put on. I would often leave the plate in such a blind rage that I could not even hear what was said to me, and occasionally did not realize who said it. I was ready to knock over anything that stood in my way or demolish whatever I could lay my hands on. I lost count of the number of bats I broke and my feet were often sore from kicking the water cooler. And the names I called myself often curled the ears of the fans who sat too close.

There is a fine lady named Mrs. Blackburn who always sits in a box right beside the dugout and she sort of adopted me. Every day she would reach over and hand me candy or chewing gum, realizing I guess that I had not outgrown my schoolboy addiction to such stuff and perhaps understanding too that I could stand the sound of a friendly voice. But I lost her one day, after she had heard me work out my vocabulary on myself coming back to the dugout after a strike-out. You understand this was no ordinary string of mild hells and damns but a whole lot of villainous Oklahoma obscenity, of the sort you might hear when somebody injured himself in the mine.

One day when I was stamping back to the dugout in a red haze, I called myself two or three of the choicest and foulest names I had ever heard used. And I was in no mood to modulate my voice. This time Mrs. Blackburn had had too much.

"Stop that talk!" she cried. I looked up almost blindly, not caring at the moment who she was or where I was and conscious only that I had added one more disgraceful strike-out to my growing string. I fixed my eye on her briefly, almost blinded by my anger.

"You shut your ——— mouth!" I told her. Almost instantly I realized what I had done and I could have chewed off my tongue. Instead I went into the dugout and fetched the water cooler an extra kick. The next time I got within earshot of Mrs. Blackburn, she called me over grimly.

"Any more outbursts like that," she told me in an icy voice, "and I am going to make a personal protest to Mr. Topping."

This really chilled me. I was still close enough to my school days to dread having to go into the principal's office for a reprimand and I promised myself, and Mrs. Blackburn, to keep my mouth tight closed after a strike-out. I did manage pretty well too, although I really shook up that water cooler.

Casey never called me on my hitting. He let me bunt when I pleased and run when I pleased. Plenty of times I have heard him snarl orders to other batters to butcher-boy the pitch if they could not hit any other way. He always accompanied that advice with a chopping motion of an imaginary bat, to show how he wanted the ball bounced through the infield. But he left me alone, except for what advice he gave me about playing the rebounds. And the only really detailed advice he gave me on that score he offered before our pre-season exhibition game at Ebbets Field. It was the first time I had played against concrete fences. As I have already recounted, I had missed the exhibition at Yankee Stadium because the draft board in my home town, having read all the newspaper stories about the home runs I was hitting, felt called upon to summon me back to make sure I really was 4-F. I was still 4-F and had been since somebody kicked me in the ankle in a football game and started an inflammation that never entirely subsided. It did not slow me down or produce unbearable pain, but it was there and it would flare up if I stayed too long on my feet.

My study of outfield fences, except at Ebbets Field, was limited to my trying to find fences I could not drive balls over. Traveling with the Yankees before the season opened, I had sent long hits over fences in San Francisco, in Hollywood, in Oakland, in Los Angeles, as well as in the training camp at Phoenix. In Los Angeles they had a small brick building next to the bleachers in Wrigley Field and I bounced a ball off that. In Hollywood I put a lot of batting-practice pitches out into the Boulevard and generally I got fat on all those nice springtime fast balls.

I think this pre-season success, and all the publicity that went with it, contributed to the letdown that struck me in Boston when I ran up against Walter Masterson in mid-July. But back with the Yankees in August, I was still striking out more than I should have and I was doing a lot of things wrong in the outfield still. They had me in right field, where hard chances are fewer and where Joe DiMaggio ranged on my meat-hand side to cover what sections of the grass I could not get to.

I don't doubt that Joe, if he had had to, could have covered the whole field, from foul line to foul line, with what he knew about the hitters and with the swiftness with which he could skim over the sod. He coached me continually, telling me how to position myself for certain hitters and certain pitches, to help the pitcher accomplish what he was trying to do, and to look over my shoulder at a ball I was running back for. Joe surely made my life easier, and I was at the top of my speed then and I am sure I could have outraced him in a straight competition. Only I could not get the jump he could on a fly ball, or line it up so quickly. Joe occasionally let me move onto his turf to take balls he could have caught easily, just to give me the practice I needed at taking balls on the run.

I was throwing too quickly and too flat-footedly, in the style of an infielder, too often forgetting the cut-off man and not always getting the distance my strong arm should have been delivering. But these were faults I was working on, with Tommy Henrich's help, and some of Casey's. I think it used to fret Casey that I enjoyed throwing knuckle balls in practice. I had been a pitcher in high school but had no desire to become one now, nor any skill either, except that I did become very adept at putting that knuckle ball where I wanted it. Casey felt that practicing this pitch, with its unnatural motion, was going to spoil my arm; but I don't believe it did, and I had too much fun with it to give it up. After a few seasons I used to keep myself in Cokes by betting all my mates they could not catch my knuckler in five straight attempts.

But to get back to Ebbets Field, where I played my first New York exhibition games. I know I gladdened Casey's heart there by hitting three singles and a home run that went over the scoreboard. That must have been the point at which Casey decided to let me be my own boss at the plate. He often had advice for the other batters but not for me. Or at least not until well into the season, when his patience finally gave out one day and he blurted a suggestion that made me think.

Usually, when I came back steaming after a strike-out, Casey's eyes would be fixed far beyond me, at the diamond, even at the fence. But once, while batting left-handed, I hauled off on three high, inside pitches and missed each one by the width of my hand, almost breaking my back in the process. This time when I returned to the bench, Casey could hold himself in no longer.

"Gahdamnit!" he growled. "You *know* you can't hit that pitch! Why the hell don't you leave it alone?"

It seems funny now that I had never thought of that solution. I had just figured that I would keep trying harder and harder to find that pitch and that someday I would learn to pickle it. But to leave it alone! Well, that turned out to be the answer. Often it went by for a ball, and I was better off for ignoring it. Of course, it would sometimes look just as fat as ever to me and I could not resist trying to drive it out of sight. But in general I avoided it and began to cut down on my strike-outs.

Actually I was not much of a man for taking advice. In school and out I had had different people tell me how to improve my batting and I quickly realized that many of them did not know what they were talking about. I knew my own strength and weaknesses better than anyone, I knew how I liked to stand in the box, and I knew the sort of bat that felt best to me. After a time Casey began to urge me to bunt more, to get out of a slump, but that had been my own idea to start with and I usually felt confident of my ability to drive the balls a long way. I am sure, from what I heard, that Casey would have liked me to try for base-hits rather than distance sometimes, but he never bugged me about this. At the plate I was my own man.

Success at the plate made me headstrong in some things. I was suspicious of any suggestion that might cause me to do differently in any way, to change my stance, my rhythm, or my luck—although I was not really superstitious. I would not even wear a batting helmet, despite Casey's pleadings, until the rules said that everybody had to. I never had any fear of getting hit in the head, because, as a switch-hitter, I knew that a ball coming at me was not going to curve away, and so I wasted no time in getting out of there. When pitchers threw at me, they eventually threw at my legs, where I was vulnerable. I wore a protective shield on my inflamed ankle part of the time, but that did not interfere with my movements at all.

The fans kept me from getting my ego too inflated. Mrs. Blackburn, and a few others, used to tell me how well I was doing and what a great player I was going to be. But there were others who seemed to feel it their job to remind me I was no Joe DiMaggio and that I was not even living up to my advance billing. For a while I enjoyed the fans, and even the kids who crowded around after my autograph and I felt it my duty to sign all the books they shoved at me, or accept and mail all the postcards they put in my hands for my signature.

But gradually it got so it was an hour's work or more

just to get through the gang at the door. And I was especially disillusioned when I noticed the same kids back there again and again after the same autograph. Their faces became as familiar to me as those of my teammates and I began to work out ways of ducking them. Usually their response to this was to take their fountain pens (this was before everybody used a ballpoint) and flip them so they splattered ink on my clothes. I had begun to fuss over my sports jackets and it really burned me to get back to my room with two or three rows of inkspots down my front, or with one lapel torn almost loose by some souvenir-crazy kid.

I don't know what it was (or is) that makes these kids think they own a piece of you, and sends even grownups into a frenzy to rip off a bit of souvenir. How do they score points that way? Is there a market for torn bits of an athlete's clothing? Or will they save them and brag to their grandchildren how they helped rip the suit off the back of some guy who used to hit a baseball long distances? I sometimes hope their grandchildren ask, "What's a baseball, grampa?"

When people ask me for an autograph, someplace where it is convenient to give it, I will hand it out, even sign a dozen pieces of paper. I posed for thousands of pictures for people decent enough to ask in advance. But I quickly lost sympathy for these young hyenas who would demand your autograph in one breath and in the next breath scream that you were a bum for not hitting home runs every trip to the plate.

Yankee Stadium is peculiar in that it seems to draw a large faction of anti-Yankee fans, who come to yell for the other side, no matter who it may happen to be, and boo the Yankees. The outfield fans, especially in the years after the war, handed out verbal abuse that would have started a fight in a Bowery barroom. And some of them used to delight to torture players by snapping small missiles at them with rubber bands or bean shooters. When I was being built up in the papers as the new Mr. Yankee, I always brought down the biggest storm of boos. These never did bother me in the least. The dirty names and the missiles were something else.

But I had plenty to comfort me. My eyes were still popping a little at the sight of the cities we visited. I have already mentioned how, when I first came to Washington, for the opening games that were never played, I actually had to tell myself out loud that it was really me, and that I was really here in the capital of the country, seeing the lighted dome of the Capitol and the Washington Monument, and the honest-to-goodness White House where lived a real live President, and I used to long for someone to tell about these things. I could not talk to my teammates, because they would have thought I was nuts.

New York was too much for me to take in, even in a whole summer. It took me long enough to learn that Brooklyn was New York, and the Bronx was New York and Times Square was also New York. The idea of ever finding my way around in the city was beyond my grasp. If it had not been for Hank Bauer I probably would never have eaten a meal in any restaurant except the Stage Delicatessen, nor have wandered more than a block or two in any direction, except to get to the Stadium.

If you've never been through a spell of shyness yourself, you can have no idea how it can choke you up and contain you, how it can force you to swallow the words that form in your heart without ever saying them, how it can make you seem sulky and egotistical and rude when you are really squirming with embarrassment over your inability to utter a polite phrase, and how it seems to feed on itself, making you more withdrawn when you are trying hardest to escape.

You get so you seek out the familiar spots, where you will make the least show of yourself when you look for a corner to light in, and you order the familiar foods over and over, rather than ask a question, or prompt a chuckle or even a raised eyebrow, or get into an explanation, or in any way prolong the small ordeal. It seemed to me I was always on the verge of saying something stupid or countrified, so I held my tongue among strangers and preferred familiar faces around me.

It was not just shyness that hampered me. I was also still a small-town boy, despite my swing around the country's major cities, and big-city ways and some aspects of lavish living were hard for me to adjust to. I remember that, when I first came back into the Yankee clubhouse after a workout on the field, I set out to take my spikes off before walking across that carpeted floor. Fortunately, some others moved through the door just ahead of me and trod spikes and all straight to their lockers, so I dared to follow. But even then I walked with extra delicacy, still half afraid that someone might complain that I was marking up the carpet.

My success with my bat helped me a great deal, of course. People are ready to forgive you anything, even what seems like rudeness, if you are making a score in the world. My inability to make small talk with the sportswriters did not injure me, because they had to interview me and the photographers had to take my picture, whether they thought me stuck up or not.

It was not that I was not enjoying myself, for I was, and every day I found myself able to thrust my neck a little further out of my shell, at least with my teammates. I was knocking in runs and stealing bases and bringing joy to Stengel's heart, so that he was always offering kind words about me, sometimes in my hearing.

Casey seemed to think more of my speed than of my power. He would nearly burst with joy to have me run out an infield hit, or drag a bunt or steal a base and, as I said, he kept urging me to do it more often. I once heard him tell someone that if I had been batting in the old days against the dead ball, I'd have made first base every time I topped a pitch. It is a fact that I had never found anyone in baseball who could outrun me. I could get a quick start and I loved to run, just as Casey and the fans loved to see me go. Fans react joyfully to aggressive baseball and Casey made it a religion. He wanted you to start scheming for that extra base while you were still in the on-deck circle, sizing up outfielders, noting their positions and moves, studying the pitcher, and going over the signs in your mind.

I liked aggressive play myself. One of my many reasons for admiring Hank Bauer was his complete unwillingness to quit, no matter what the score or what the situation. There was never a play he was involved in when he did not give his fiercest effort. And when Casey kept him on the bench, he steamed like a kettle. Hank could play any position on the diamond and had done so. He pitched and played the infield and outfield in the minors and in a pinch, once, he went behind the bat for the Yankees. To me he was the complete ballplayer, and still is. I hope I caught a little of his feeling that winning is what makes baseball fun. I know I have admired him all my life.

But I never actually imitated or tried to model myself after any baseball player. I was always a bug on doing things my own way—perhaps a little too much so at times. Still, if you start shifting your stance or changing your method of taking off on a steal, you are bound to affect your confidence, and confidence is the one ingredient you cannot get through imitation. You get that through accomplishment, and through feeling relaxed and comfortable at the plate, on the bases, and in the field. It is confidence that makes you give a desperate try for the balls you have only a slight chance of catching. And it is confidence that enables you to stand up to a pitcher who struck you out last time up and wallop his best pitch into the seats.

I say I have never imitated any ballplayer, but there is one whose general attitude at the plate I have tried to acquire. That is Ted Williams, who was the best batter I ever saw in action. Ted showed me what it means to be aggressive at the plate. When he decided to go after a ball, he really attacked it, as if he meant to demolish it entirely. There was never anything defensive about his ways at the plate, no halfhearted swings or pokes. He exploded at a ball, trying to drive it as hard and as far

I was about three years old when this was taken and my father was twenty-two. I simply couldn't imagine a stronger or braver man than he was. *(Brown Brothers)*

When I played for Miami (Oklahoma). I had just turned fourteen. *(UPI)*

The whole family was in on this card game, except my sister Barbara. My brother Butch and my mother are kibitzing. *(UPI)*

When I played for Joplin (Mo.). I was only eighteen and never dreamed I would be with the Yankees the very next season. Joplin was Class C. *(UPI)*

NY

My brothers Roy and Ray, who are twins, starred with the Commerce High School football team when I was with the Yankees. Here are the twin halfbacks with me before a workout on the high school field. *(UPI)*

This was the most thrilling day in my life—when Merlyn and I cut the wedding cake together at her parents' home in Picher, Oklahoma. *(UPI)*

When I came home to Commerce, after my second season with the Yankees, they could not get my Yankee cap away from me. *(Brown Brothers)*

I think this picture was taken on my first trip to Phoenix with the Yankees. If it was, then I probably threw that baseball into the seats. *(Brown Brothers)*

I was grinning in this picture because this was the day when I finally returned to the Yankees to stay, after being sent back to Kansas City. Casey grinned later on because I hit a home run that day to help beat Cleveland. *(UPI)*

Here was the blackest moment in my life up to that time. I tripped over an outfield drain and thought my leg was broken and my career finished. This was in the 1951 World Series. That's Joe DiMaggio coming up. *(UPI)*

You'll notice that I have a tendency to uppercut the ball when I bat lefty, and when I meet the ball my weight has shifted to my front foot. *(Marvin E. Newman)*

Yankees

In dragging a bunt the idea is to get out of there at top speed once you have laid the ball down. Sometimes I took off so fast that I carried the bat part way to first base. Rounding a base, when the ball is behind you, it is a good idea to take a quick flash back to see what's happening to it.
(Marvin E. Newman)

This catch made Don Larsen happy because it saved his perfect game in the 1956 World Series. It is an example of what confidence can do. If you keep your eye on the ball and tell yourself you can catch it, you'll be surprised sometimes at the catches you make. *(UPI)*

This will give you an idea of how I feel when the Yankees are winning. At the time, nothing else seems to matter. *(Marvin E. Newman)*

Mickey Junior was thirteen when he came to spring training with me. He never had any ambition to become a ballplayer and I did not force him. But he is a great golfer.
(Wide World)

NEW YOR

When the 1966 season opened I was hoping I might get back into form after my operation. I was glad to be back and I guess the kids were glad to see me. *(Wide World)*

The manager I most admire is Ralph Houk, shown here in 1966 before the season opened, and before I found out that I was not going to be able to play regularly. *(Wide World)*

Just before the operation on my shoulder, I was feeling pretty cheerful because the doctors had told me they could probably fix me so I could throw again. *(Wide World)*

You can get an idea from the look on my face how uneasy I was when I first started to work out at first base. It's a lot easier now, and I'm mighty glad I gave it a try.
(Wide World)

as he could. I know that is not the way for every batter. But it was the right way for Ted and me.

One thing that made my life a great deal pleasanter that first season in New York was the anticipation of picking up a full World Series share in the fall. To me that would mean just about an extra year's salary and it made it certain that Merlyn and I would get married. Cleveland was breathing on the Yankees' neck that season and it took some of the best pitching I ever saw, a no-hit game by Allie Reynolds, to make sure that we would come in first. This was Allie's second no-hitter of the season (he had pitched one just before I was sent down to Kansas City) and it helped convince me that I belonged to the greatest ball club in the world.

My memory about my own great deeds in that first season is happily rather dim, and I will never be tempted to bore my grandsons with the details of my first home run, or my longest, because I honestly recall very little about them. Memory for details, as a matter of fact, is an in-and-out thing with me. I remember stuff that I might better forget—dumb mistakes I made, minor celebrations, a glove I was fond of. But the important things leak right through my brain like sand through a sieve. Not too long ago, for instance, I was asked in a legal proceeding if I had received a check for $90,000. Determined to answer honestly, I said I did not remember. And that was the simple truth. It perhaps sounds put-on to say that a sum like that is of no account to me. But that's not it at all. I remember smaller sums of money, like the price of the baseball glove my father bought me. But I just could not remember that big beautiful check. The legal eagles at the proceeding made it clear they thought I was being evasive, and ridiculed the very notion of forgetting such a chunk of wealth. I was ready to grant that I must have got the check. But I just could not bring back to mind ever holding the check in my hand.

And so I cannot answer questions about many of the home runs I hit. What was the first one in a big league park? It must have been one at Ebbets Field, but what sort of pitch it was or where it went I could never say now. There are home runs I do remember, but for special reasons that have nothing to do with their historical interest.

This first year I spent a lot of time just getting used to my sudden fame and my imminent wealth—or to the idea of them—and getting used to big-city life. The things that were important to me then are of so little consequence now that it is hard to realize they ever used to occupy my mind. I know that I made an effort to win over the fans occasionally, perhaps thinking that if I would indicate my own good will toward them, they might reciprocate and ease up on the riding they gave me.

One day, after I had picked off a fungo fly and was ready to trot in to the bench, I tossed the ball into the nearby stands, where the kids could scramble for it. I trotted in then, well pleased with myself and with the happy response the kids gave me. Later that afternoon, however, I was invited in to see Mr. Weiss, whom I had never talked to except briefly when Casey brought me in to agree on a contract. I had no notion of what was brewing, but I was always uneasy in this man's presence. I always felt like a schoolboy in the principal's office when I had to talk to him.

This time he wanted to talk to me about throwing baseballs into the stands!

"In the first place," he told me, "the balls are not yours to give away. They belong to the club. In the second place, you may very well hurt somebody that way and find yourself in a damage suit. So don't do it again."

I was really speechless. Not entirely from embarrassment but because I honestly had never dreamed that a club like the Yankees would be chintzy about baseballs. The general atmosphere around there had struck me as open-handed, opulent, and damn-the-expense. Carpets on the locker-room floor! Wide upholstered sofa and chairs to lounge in! Free stationery and writing desk! Luxurious big towels by the ton! And still the general manager had time to fret over a free baseball!

Later on I realized that he was right about the damage suit and that it was this rather than the free baseball that had disturbed him. He gave me the bit about not owning the baseball because he probably thought it would make more sense to my juvenile mind. Instead it made me tab him as stingy and it sent me into salary negotiations every spring with a conviction that I was going to be squeezed. Come to think of it, it may all have been part of the psychological warfare so I would be more readily satisfied with any raise I got.

That first year, however, I found nothing to kick about in my salary, especially with that World Series money in view. My tastes had not yet fully developed and so I could not think of many things I wanted to spend money on. My father was earning more money in the mines than ever before—about $100 a week—and it seemed to me that the Mantle family was finally walking on Easy Street.

This conviction that everything was coming our way made the blow that fell that fall all the more devastating. I think a lot of boys who have not been brought up rich develop the same sort of subconscious feeling that I must have had—that sudden success is bound to be short-lived, that big money cannot last, and that something is bound to happen when the balloon grows too big. I don't mean that I ever really harbored any such feeling, but it must have been there deep inside me just the same.

All went well until the World Series. I was suffering through my strike-outs, but I was always compensating for them with a long blow or two, so that I managed to run my RBI total to sixty-five for ninety games. My family came East for my first World Series and everything tasted twice as good to me to know that my father was going to be in the stands for all the games, it being a subway series, with the ball parks just a subway stop away from each other.

Perhaps it was from trying too hard that I failed to accomplish anything in the first World Series game, played on October 4th at Yankee Stadium. Or maybe this old-timer the Giants used for starter—left-handed Dave Koslo, age thirty-one—was just too crafty for me. Anyway, I collected a horse-collar that game and made up my mind that next time out I was going to get a World Series hit, even if I had to do it with a bunt. Luckily we had a right-hander pitching against us in the second game—Larry Jansen—and so I was batting left-handed. Leading off in the first inning, I dragged a bunt and made first with steps to spare. Phil Rizzuto pushed a bunt too and sent me to second. Then McDougald dumped a humpbacked drive right over second base where no one could reach it and I tore right on home, to score my first World Series run. I knew my father would be celebrating it in the stands and I could not have been happier. Next time up I tried for the touchdown and made out, but I still felt that I could hit this pitcher, sharp as he was. Then the axe fell.

It all came about so foolishly, and might so easily never have happened, that if I were inclined to be superstitious I might think it was fated that way. Willie Mays hit a high fly to right center. It was not a difficult play and not even in my territory. Joe DiMaggio had it lined up immediately and I was just sprinting over to back him up and I guess to look like a ballplayer. I had seen these little drains that were buried in the outfield grass and had avoided them before. This time I just got my spikes in the wooden covering of one and it threw me. As I went down, all 175 pounds in a heap, I heard a sort of cracking noise from my knee and I was convinced I had broken my leg. The pain was sharp but it was not overpowering. But I lay absolutely motionless on the grass. Some people said I had passed out from pain. Some thought I had suffered a heart attack and dropped dead. Joe DiMaggio thought I had been shot. But two things held me immobilized. The noise that had come from my knee and the excruciating hurt I felt convinced me that I had broken my leg and would never play baseball again. And I think some subconscious childish impulse prompted me to lie quite still with the idea that if I pretended it had not happened it might go away. Secondly, I had heard somewhere that you should never move your body when a bone is broken, lest you splinter it irreparably, and I think this too may have urged me to lie without moving a muscle. What I felt most like doing was crying. And I sure needed my father's sympathy, and I wished he were at my side.

In very short order he was. Men ran out from the bench to minister to me and the report that my knee was probably not broken helped diminish the black panic that had overwhelmed me. I was carried off then on a stretcher, like a side of beef, and ticketed for the hospital. My father got in the cab with me and Dr. Gaynor, and all the way back to the hotel he assured me that I would be all right, that it was good if it had to happen it had happened at the season's end, and that a long rest would make the leg strong as new. To understand the tragedy that lay ahead, you have to realize that my father had always been the strongest figure in my life. It was he I tried always to please and he I always counted on to rescue me from trouble or danger and watch over me if I was sick. And he always looked the part of a muscular, vigorous, dependable, and strong-willed man whom no fear could faze and no enemy overcome.

The next morning we taxied to the hospital, where I was to be X-rayed. I had to slide out of the cab and try to maneuver on my good leg. My father got out first and reached in to steady me. Once on the sidewalk, I put my arm around his iron shoulders and leaned all my weight on him. Without a sound he crumpled right to the sidewalk beneath my weight.

It was as if my own legs had turned to lard. Shaken with fright, I held myself steady on the cab and waited for the doctor to help my father to his feet. My father confessed to not feeling well, and the doctor saw quickly that he had two patients rather than one. I was ready to believe that some transient illness had given my father a dizzy spell, but I was deeply troubled all the same.

We were bedded down side by side in the hospital,

with a television set at our feet where we both could watch the rest of the Series. Meanwhile, the doctors were testing my father to see what had weakened him, and their vague cheerfulness made me more and more uneasy. Within a short time I knew the worst: My father had Hodgkin's disease, probably well advanced, and was desperately in need of treatment.

I had never heard of Hodgkin's disease, but I knew what it meant when they explained it was a form of cancer. At that moment the only thing the World Series meant to me was a God-sent supply of extra cash, enough, I promised myself, to get my father the very best medical treatment the country supplied, to make him all well again. I could not believe that, if you had the money to pay for it, you could not buy a cure for just about anything. And it was still impossible for me to connect my father, still alert, still immersed in his interest in the Series, still primarily concerned for my own health—to connect him with anything like dying.

Merlyn and I got married that winter and together we took my father out to the Mayo Brothers Clinic and promised him that we would have all the money he needed to make him well again. I don't know if he believed it or not. I think it is hard to put out the spark of optimism in a man of my father's nature. And I think that, in spite of what the doctors told me, I was infected with my father's cheerfulness too. It just did not seem possible that anyone with that much will to live would be downed except by years and years of illness.

The doctors at the clinic told me solemnly that my father was not going to be cured, that his symptoms might be alleviated but that his disease was well advanced and his life expectancy probably measurable in months. They told him he could go back to work if he pleased or could conserve what strength he had to lengthen his life, as long as there was no need for his income to keep the family fed. I had already learned that he had been sick for months—had recently had to sleep sitting up. But neither my mother nor he had wanted to worry me.

My father's own courage sustained him and all the rest of us. He did manage to persuade us, if not himself, that he believed a cure could be found and that he was not going to give up. Again his own outlook infected me and before long he had me believing that, if we kept on looking for treatment, we might fool the doctors yet. It had been done, I had heard, and my father had none of the air of a dying man about him.

Except for his longing to live to see "a redheaded grandson," I do not believe my father was ever concerned with himself. Eventually the disease began to lay its mark on him. He lived until spring. But first he took himself off to a sanitarium in Denver. He persuaded my mother, who went with him, that there was help to be found there, a new treatment of some sort that might bring a little hope.

But I know the true reason was that he did not want my sister and younger brothers to see him waste away. He became very conscious of the effect his appearance had on them. And to all those who knew him in his strength it was frightening, almost like watching a man turn into a skeleton. It was typical of him to be concerned for his family more than for himself, and he always owned the courage that enabled him to meet every sort of distress as if it were his job to cope with it, without hollering for help.

But the winter immediately following the diagnosis of his illness was not an unhappy one. It was easy to share his own calm optimism and to settle into the enjoyment of whatever time he had left. After Merlyn and I got married, the whole world looked so bright to me I just could not believe that my father was really as ill as the doctors had said. I could see the signs of his increasing weakness; but I am sure he concealed many of his symptoms from all of us.

The doctors had told me I must put no undue strain on my knee. But married man or no, I was still not completely mature and I had the bullheadedness typical of most strong adolescents. I just refused to accept even the slightest form of invalidism when I felt so good all over. And if I *felt* good, how could anything be wrong?

So I accepted invitations to play basketball in the high-school gymnasium now and then and, of course, before long, what with the sudden stops and starts and quick change of direction this game requires, I twisted my knee once more, so when spring training came around, I was just a slight bit gimpy. And from that gimpiness I think followed many of the ailments that have dogged me season after season.

Favoring that knee forced me from time to time to move or stand awkwardly, with the result that the other knee grew sore and eventually weakened. And the condition of my legs sometimes prevented me from doing all the conditioning exercises I should have. As a result I injured other muscles or acquired pulls and strains in arms and back that ordinarily I might have escaped. Some of these ailments may be traced to my stubborn refusal to follow good advice or from a natural desire to do what I could for the club, despite what I sometimes thought of as trifling aches and pains.

Then there was another motive that I think athletic coaches are sometimes inclined to overlook—that was the natural urge every young athlete feels to play the games he is good at. For the first six or seven years at least I could hardly wait for spring training to begin, and once I was in camp, I had trouble holding myself in check when everybody else was working out on the diamond. It is normal, I think, for young fellows to make light of the dire warnings of their elders concerning the future damage that may result from ignoring advice. But it is also nearly impossible for a young man who has not had his fill of baseball to postpone his participation in the game when it is being played right under his nose. The time does come when the game becomes work and it requires an effort of will to push yourself through the grind of training and put up with all the strains of a long, hard schedule. Then, however, there is the need to help the club win ball games, and that will sometimes prompt you to conceal, even from yourself, the true extent of an injury.

From this variety of motives, at any rate, I kept doing the things that prevented me from ever growing 100 per cent sound in the legs and back, so I never did contribute to the club everything I wanted to, and perhaps could have.

People talk about the evils of making heroes out of athletes, and the manner in which young egos are swelled by too much success and too much acclamation when you are young. I am sure I suffered a little from too much praise at the beginning, but not because it made my head swell. My father's training prevented that. What it did do was give me impossible ideals to try to live up to, and exaggerated notions of what was expected of me, so that, in my early years with the Yankees, I sometimes pressed too hard to deliver the mighty blow that would demolish the opposition.

But there is another side to this star business that the observers I have listened to never mention—that is the sense of responsibility that goes with it. One of the great things about baseball is that it helps you submerge your own private aims in a team effort to win. It gets so you actually forget your own hurts at times, so strong is the desire to help your club—the men you work and play with every day—come out on top. And if you are carrying the big batting average and delivering the most runs, you are ashamed to nurse your bruises on the bench when the rest of the club desperately needs you. Being a star or a near-star makes you feel that the other fellows depend on you to keep the club winning and so you have a strong urge all the time to get into the line-up and contribute what you can. This urge, believe me, can be stronger than the urge to save yourself so your career may be longer, and stronger than the desire to protect yourself from injury.

Also you develop, or I know I developed, a feeling of

obligation to the kids who are never going to get into the big money, who may not even last long enough to qualify for the pension plan, and who still give the game all they've got on the baselines, in the field, and at the plate. The fact is that without them you would not even be earning your own salary. If you can help them earn a World Series cut or even help them pick up a few bucks for an advertising endorsement or something, you get some satisfaction out of doing it.

I know there have been athletic stars so concerned with their own records or their own salary demands or the preservation of their own precious strength that they just refuse to put out when conditions are not exactly right. But they never belonged on the Yankees, and I don't believe any of them ever really hit the top, or went as far as they might have. Even Ty Cobb, who was supposed to have been the most individualistic of them all and had many a row with his teammates, still, according to men who knew him, was ready to risk a broken leg any time to help his club come in first. Babe Ruth and Joe DiMaggio too had this ability to submerge themselves in the team effort to come out on top and both of them played ball with sore arms and bad legs when they felt the club needed them.

So I am not going to complain about the ailments that kept me from setting the records that some of the fans and writers thought I should be setting. I know I aggravated my own ailments by not being as careful as I might have. But I also know that many of the other players made their own contributions without concerning themselves with their aches and pains. This is not to say that I was not foolish about straining that gimpy leg before I should have. I know I was, and I blame that foolhardiness for most of the other troubles that beset me in later years.

LESSON THREE

Confidence, the secret ingredient of all athletic skill, is built on accomplishment. When I started hitting baseballs left-handed and right-handed, 400 feet and more, in the ball parks at Phoenix and San Francisco and Hollywood, I knew in my heart that I could hit big league pitching just as I had the minor league stuff. And so I walked to the plate in Ebbets Field and in Yankee Stadium with far less nervousness than I experienced walking for the first time into a big-city restaurant. But as success builds confidence, failure washes it away. It took just a succession of strike-outs and a sudden expression of what I felt was non-confidence by the manager to start me tensing up at the plate and letting pitches go by that I might have turned into base-hits. Instead of dwelling on all the solid hits I had made, in parks all over the country, I began to listen to the inner voice that had always told me that I should never have taken a chance in going so far from home, that I was not old enough or big enough to play in this league, and that *somebody* ought to feel sorry for me.

If anyone but my father had upbraided me as he did, it would not have helped. But he reminded me that I had not really lost my skills at all and that I was going to have to work out this problem for myself. When I looked bad in other men's eyes, I always knew I could count on my father for sympathy. But when I looked bad to *him*—well, I knew I had reached the end of the alley and would have to turn right back and fight whatever it was that had scared me. It turned out that there was nothing to be afraid of at all. Many a man, when he runs into a corner and finds he has to turn and face his enemy, discovers he can lick the enemy after all. So confidence can be born of desperation too—the knowledge that you have nothing more to lose by trying your best to do what you have done before. That is why managers advise you, when you are in a slump, to keep swinging. If you start to get cozy, to hold back until you are *sure* you won't miss, you just diminish your chances. And if you begin to lunge at the ball, to flail wildly in an effort to get back in the groove, the slump is going to get deeper and deeper.

One thing you should keep in mind: Nobody loses his batting skill overnight. It may be, as in my case, that the pitchers discover one pitch that you cannot hit well and keep feeding it to you. It may be that overconfidence prompts you to fall into a careless manner at the plate. It may be that one taste of power—like a grand-slam home run—gets you to swinging at everything within reach, so that you forget your strike zone. But whatever happens, the skill is still there, and all you have to do is use patience and persistence to get it back. Go up to the plate every time telling yourself that you can hit this guy no matter what he throws. Then make him throw what *you* want.

Carelessness at the plate is not the same as being relaxed. You want to be relaxed. But you do not want to let your mind wander over past failures or past successes, or over what part of the stands you will put the ball into, or over what you may do after the game. You must get your eye on the ball and keep it there, concentrating with every last fragment of your brain on the job of meeting the ball with the bat, and watching the ball, every pitch, all the way in, whether you swing at it or not. If you catch yourself pressing—lunging out after the ball and swinging off balance—step out of the box and get hold of yourself. There's no rush about swinging. You can afford to wait for your pitch at least until there's a strike on you. Look at what the pitcher is offering and decide how you are going to deal with him. Watch the ball! Watch the ball!

Watch it go back to the pitcher and keep your eye on it all the time it is in his hands. This sort of concentration, plus the confidence that enables you to go back to the plate after a strike-out and belt a ball into the bleachers—they are what will make you into a real hitter.

My idea of confidence personified will always be Johnny Mize. Johnny, after he had apparently played out a full lifetime in the National League, joined the Yankees in 1949, when he was thirty-six years old. When I joined the Yankees, big John was still there, crowding forty now, playing first base from time to time and pinch-hitting. He would stroll up to the plate as if he were taking his turn at the barber's and would stand there so relaxed it did not seem possible he would ever get the bat around. Once in a while he would flex both knees, to make sure of his stance. Then, when he found a pitch he liked, he would lash at it as fiercely as any man I ever saw.

John also was an illustration of what I said about not losing your batting skills overnight. No one could deny that John had seen better days in the field. He was far from spry around first base. The Giants had let him go and no one else in the league had wanted him. Yet he put in nearly five seasons with the Yankees and was still able to deliver a home run to win a ball game when it was needed most.

It should go without saying that lots of practice is essential. Swinging that bat day in and day out helps you develop all the skills you need—your timing, your strength, your confidence. Some men, as I said, even use an old auto tire or some such object hung on a rope and work out by whacking that in the off-season, the way a boxer works out on the heavy bag to get strength into his wallop and to get the feeling of hitting something solid. I want to repeat my belief in lots of bunting practice. Some players, and even some managers, think bunting comes easy and needs no attention. But there are others, like Hank Bauer, who have their charges putting in long stretches of nothing but bunting. It takes practice to learn just what sort of tap to deliver to a ball to get it out where it can't be fielded right away. It also takes practice to learn how to hold the bat—not too tight and not too loose—so that the ball will drop to the ground and not carom off into the air, or pop right back to the pitcher.

Aggressive baseball, which was the subject Casey taught

best, has largely to do with hitting. But it includes base-running too and it means constant mental concentration. He used to take a player right from the bench, to the on-deck circle, to the plate and around the bases to illustrate just what sort of thinking and planning and play a man could engage in at every point in the trip. On the bench, he wanted you to watch the pitcher. Many times it is possible, if you keep your eye on the ball as the pitcher makes ready to deliver it, to pick up some little fault, some habit of posture or windup, that will tip off the pitches. You can also learn, by watching, what the pitching pattern is likely to be—what the man depends on when he is behind the hitter, what pitch he uses for his waste pitch. Base-runners especially can learn a great deal from studying pitchers, especially when there is a runner on base. They can sometimes discover just what the difference may be between the move to first and the move the pitcher uses when he is really going to pitch to the plate. Of course the best pitchers have these moves worked out so there is no telling. But once in a while you may find a pitcher who gives himself away without knowing it—by the way he fingers the ball in the glove, by the way his elbows contract or his feet are placed. Knowledge like this can give you a winning jump on a pitcher, which is what you need in order to steal a base.

When you are in the on-deck circle, next at bat, you can first go over all the signs in your mind. Make sure you know exactly what the bunt sign is and what the steal and take signs may be. Most managers send a hitter to the plate hitting—except in special situations—and give him a sign if he is to let a pitch go by. These signs may change from day to day—may be given one way for the first five men in the order and another way for the last four. And there is always a take-off sign, to indicate that the sign just given no longer applies. This you have to be sure you know. You review these things quickly while you are on deck and if you are in doubt about any of them, you check with the coach before you go to bat.

You also begin, if you are playing aggressive Stengel-type baseball, to decide beforehand what you may do if the batter ahead of you gets on base. Will you be called upon for a sacrifice? Do you understand the hit-and-run sign that you may have with this batter? Then go over in your mind the abilities of the fielders you will be facing. If you hit to center, as you usually do, what sort of arm has the man got? Is he right-handed or left-handed? Where does he play you? Is his arm in shape today, or have you seen evidence of a sore arm?

The answers to these questions help you decide, if you hit the ball, whether or not you can go for that extra base. Once you get to bat, you check the positions of the fielders. When you hit the ball, you will know if they are deep or shallow, and whether the ball has gone far to the right of the fielder or directly at him. While at the plate too you can observe the moves of the infielders. Do they cheat toward the base when a curve is coming? Are they in on the dirt? Back deep on the grass? Who charges for an expected bunt? Sometimes you may even fake a bunt to pick up this information. Or you may push a bunt toward second base if the man in that position is playing you deep, or push it toward third if the third baseman is playing flat-footedly, behind the baseline, and does not move in with the pitch.

Knowing in advance, without studying it after you have made your hit, just where the outfielders are will help you decide if you want to swing wide as you approach first and try for second. When you are on first base, you are alert for signs again. And again you check the fielders. This time, if the ball is hit to right, you will not have to look out there after the hit to learn if the fielder is close to the foul line, shifted toward center, is playing shallow or deep. You can dig for second, knowing just about how far the fielder will have to travel to recover the ball, or if he has any chance to catch it on the fly. On your way to second you do not have to watch your feet. Casey liked to remind base-runners that there are no deep holes on the baseline that you have to watch for, and no benches or baby carriages to steer clear of, so you can afford to glance to the outfield to see how the ball is fielded. Did it go through to the wall? Then you can swing wide as you approach second and try for third. Did the player charge it well and field it quickly? Then you have to be satisfied with one base.

When there is a runner ahead of you, you have to know

what he is up to or you may catch up to him and get yourself hung up in a rundown. If the coach is holding up the runner at third, then you have got to stop at second. Never fail to check this as you approach second base. Look for the third-base coach, about halfway down the third-base line toward home. If he is sending the preceding runner in, then you can turn on the juice. But if he is holding the man, then you have to stay on second.

A wide-awake base-runner should never be doubled on a line drive. Of course, if there are two out, you are not going to be doubled anyway. And if the hit-and-run sign has been given, you have got to start with the pitch. But even then you don't need to charge along with your head down. You can always spare a quick glance back to see if the ball is going through. Even if it does go through, you still should stay alive to the chance to take extra bases.

When you are on second, it begins again. Check the fielders. Check the coach for signs. Know exactly where the second baseman is playing, or if the center fielder is close in behind the base. The coach will be watching the shortstop and will warn you if he breaks for the base to try to trap you. You will be able to see the second baseman yourself and you should be aware all the time of just where he is playing. As a matter of fact, you should not leave it to the coach to tell you about the shortstop. You can spare an occasional quick peek at him too, to be sure he is not closer to the bag than you are. Frank Crosetti always taught us that a long lead off second is not much use anyway unless you are really a fast runner. If you take a moderate lead off the bag, and take a start when the pitch is on its way, the opposition will probably make no attempt to pick you off. But if you get too far off the bag, where you constantly have to be ready to get back, you may not get the start you need when the ball is hit. Your weight will be on the wrong foot and you may be actually on your way back to second, responding to a bluff by one of the fielders. So an average runner should not go for those big dangerous leads here. It is too easy for the shortstop to beat you back to the base.

Ground balls that are hit ahead of you usually mean that

you should hold on to second base. But before even the ball is hit, you should go over the possibilities in your mind. Is there a runner behind you? Then you will *have* to run if the ball is hit. Is first base open? Then you can hold on to the bag if you want to. If the ball is hit on the ground ahead of you, you should stay close to the bag. But stay awake just the same and watch to see if the ball goes through, or if it draws the shortstop or third baseman so far out of position that they could never make a play at third. If the ball gets away, or if the fielder obviously cannot make a play, then go ahead and help yourself to third base. Check the ball too and see if perhaps it gets by an outfielder. If it does, you have a good chance to score. In any event, you may want to turn and give a good bluff at scoring. That means that you swing out a little as you approach the bag, then go through the motions of digging hard for home. Of course, you will have to decide for yourself how far down the baseline you can go without getting trapped. The coach can't always tell you this because you know better than anyone how quickly you can move.

If the ball is hit on the ground to the first baseman or second baseman, then the chances are that you can advance (on condition, remember, that first base was open and you can't be forced). If the ball is hit on a line, you have got to keep your eye on it. Play safe until you see what happens to the ball. The manager is not going to feel sorry for you if you get doubled on a line drive caught in the infield. It is up to you to avoid being doubled by waiting to see what happens to the ball.

Often on a deep fly or long line drive you will have a chance to take third after the catch. When the ball is hit in the air to an outfielder and you are on second, you should get partway down the line, ready to go either way—to advance if the ball is dropped, to get back and tag up if it is caught. But first of all you review the situation when you are on second base. Is there one out? Then you do not want to take a chance on advancing on a short fly, or on any fly where the fielder's arm puts you in real danger. If the fly makes the second out in the inning, then it is not worth much to your club to have you on third base instead of on second. But if the fly makes the first out, then it is worth taking a chance to get over where a sacrifice or an out can bring you in.

You must also, as you stand on second, remind yourself of the score. Do you represent the tying or winning run? Then, in case of a drive to the outfield, it may be worth while to try to score. But if your club is several runs behind, then it is better to hang on to what you've got and give your club a chance to make some more hits and perhaps get a bunch of runs.

While you are on second, you can help your club sometimes by watching the catcher's signs and matching them up with the pitch. Of course, the catcher will be using a special code, with a lot of dummy signs, to keep you from picking up the pitch. But there is nothing to prevent your trying. Only don't let this study distract you from making note of where the shortstop and second baseman are. You don't want to get absent-minded on the basepaths, or someone is likely to lay a baseball on you and put you out.

As you advance from second to third, you have a number of possibilities that you ought to consider. First of all you have to check to see where the ball is and decide if you are going to try to go all the way. You cannot make this decision after you have reached third unless, of course, there is an error that provides a sudden chance to keep going. But if you think, on the basis of your own speed and what you know of the fielder's ability, that you can make it all the way home, then you make your swing as you approach the base, tag the inside corner of the base, and head straight down the baseline for home. The coach will probably go partway down the line himself so he can throw the stop sign if the ball gets back sooner than you figured. Then you must slam on the brakes and scramble back. But barring any such catastrophe, if you have made up your mind to go, then *go.* Breaking your stride to take another look at the situation may just give the fielder that extra half-second he needs to put you out at the plate. If the ball is in the hands of an infielder as you try for third—that is, if the second baseman or first baseman has handled the ball and made a play at first—then you should go straight down the baseline for the base. This will keep your body between the baseman and the ball and perhaps prevent him from fielding it clearly.

There are other things you have to concern yourself with as you stand on second base. Is there a man on third? How many out?

If there is a man ahead of you, you have to take care not to catch up with him. If there is one out, you don't want to take long chances running to third, especially on a ball that crosses the baseline ahead of you. Even if the play is made to first and the runner put out there, it still will take a base-hit to score you from third, so the advantage is not worth running a long chance. Still, you do not want to give up too easily on a ball hit in front of you. Watch it! If it goes through, be ready to move. And if it goes through between the third baseman and the baseline, you can likely go all the way, unless the left fielder was playing unusually shallow and close to the line.

Once you have reached third base, if you are playing aggressive baseball, you appraise the situation all over again. Less than two out? Then you must be ready to score on any ball hit to the outfield. Again you take a lead and watch to see if the ball is going to land safely or be caught. If it is going to be caught, and the fielder is deep enough so that you think you can beat his throw, then you must be ready to go the moment the ball touches his glove. Don't wait for the coach to send you. If you wait for word from him, there will be a split-second delay, and you need all the split seconds you can get to bring that score in. Keep one foot on the base. Start to go with the *other* foot just *before* the ball hits the fielder's glove. Then the hind foot will not leave the base until the catch is made. But you will still have a start on the play.

While you are holding third base, you always take your lead in foul territory, off on the grass, so a fair ball will not hit you and turn you into an out. You naturally run down a few steps toward home on the pitch. If the pitcher winds up, as some pitchers do when the bases are full, you can get a few extra steps. But never run down so far that you cannot scramble back to beat a pick-off throw from the catcher. You will have to decide for yourself how far down the baseline you dare advance. But when you scramble back, be sure to come back on the baseline, so that you will obstruct the catcher's view and interfere with the throw too, if he makes one.

There are other things an aggressive runner can do on third, short of scoring a run. You can, of course, help unsettle a pitcher by getting a walking start, then bluffing a steal of home. But again you have to use your head, and your knowledge of your own agility, to decide just how far down the line you dare go. Sometimes on a ground ball to a drawn-in infield you can save an out with a good bluff toward home. If you put your head down and really dig for the plate, without going too far, you may draw a throw to the plate that will let the hitter reach first safely. You cannot be halfhearted about a bluff like this, however. You have to put on a really convincing act. If you are not good at putting on the brakes and going into reverse, you can't get away with this. But if you know how to lower your tail quickly to halt your forward progress, then turn and scramble for the base, you can really help your club.

Suppose the infield is playing at normal depth. Then you must be ready to score on a ground ball. Take the lead you are allowed, then move off the base as the pitcher delivers the ball. If you start off slowly and go a little faster as the pitcher winds up (most pitchers do when the bases are full), you can be under full steam when the ball reaches the batter. But you still must be able to stop and get back if the ball goes through to the catcher. If the ball is hit on the ground, however, no one is going to get you out.

If the other bases are empty and the pitcher pitches from a stretch, you will not get this big start. You have to judge the length of your lead by the distance the third baseman is from the base. Then make a start when the pitcher releases the ball and watch to see where the ball is hit. On a fly to the outfield, unless there is an abnormally short fence that the ball may bounce off, you have to hold up to see if it will be caught, then get back to tag up if it seems that it will. Even if the fielder who catches the ball is close enough to throw you out, you may be able to make it home if you watch what he does with the ball. Give him your good bluff and if he fakes a throw, then go full tilt, for once he has made the fake, he will have a hard time catching you—*if* you have good speed, that is. If he throws to the plate, get back fast. If he throws to the relay man, wait to see what happens to the ball. It still may get away and you can always scramble back if the throw is good.

When you are on third, with a runner on first, you must be alert for the double steal. This is the maneuver that attempts to draw a throw to second when the man on first starts down. Your only hope of scoring on this play is to take off the instant the catcher uncorks his throw. If you wait until the ball is on its way, you are dead, unless somebody louses up the play. Of course, this is a gamble and your manager is not going to ask for it unless he is ready to take a chance. If the catcher is clever, as some catchers are, at bluffing a throw, he can trap you in a rundown, and that is the chance you must take. But if you do get caught in a rundown, do not surrender. Keep them working on you to give the other man a chance to advance. The more throws you force, the more chances there are that someone is going to drop the ball or throw it off target, so keep dodging back and forth, bluffing a charge at the man who holds the ball and dodging back just as long as you can.

There is an even fancier maneuver, related to the double steal, that we were able to work successfully a few times. This calls for the runner on first to try to advance to second after a short fly has been caught, when there is a man on third—assuming that the fly has made the first out. We would do this on any kind of fly, but especially on one that was far too short for the man on third to score on. As soon as the catch was made, the man on first would break for second. But the man on third would be tagged up too and moving toward home. He would break into a run as soon as the outfielder threw. If the play was made at second, the runner on third was almost sure to score. But if the outfielder anticipated the play and threw home, we would still have a man in scoring position at least.

Well, that's not all of it, but that's a sample of aggressive baseball, and it involves a good deal more than sitting on the bench waiting your turn at bat. No one on the Yankee bench was ever permitted to goof off. Everyone was busy keeping track of the score, the current situation, and the movement of the fielders. And someone always made a study of the enemy pitcher—and of our own pitcher too. You have to figure that the opposition is just as smart as you are, and if you study a pitcher, looking for giveaway moves, they'll likely be doing the same thing with your pitcher. I can remember one day when one of our pitchers was getting clobbered so steadily that Frank Crosetti decided he must be tipping off his pitches. Every time he threw a fast ball, someone landed on it. It took several innings to find out what he was doing wrong, then Cro saw it. The pitcher was looking down at his feet every time before he threw the curve. He stopped doing that and the other side stopped hitting him.

Of course, along with a study of the potentials of your situation at every base goes an aggressive spirit. A man who can start fast and can run fast should cultivate this aggressiveness—this readiness to grab an extra base or stage a realistic bluff at every opportunity. Just plain speed is never enough. As a matter of fact, some base-runners are spoiled by their own speed, and go dashing around the bases as though nothing mattered except getting as far as possible on every hit. These are the men who over-run second and third, who get caught in rundowns with two out, and who are frequently doubled up on line drives.

A club that uses aggressive tactics will often get the opposition off balance, will upset the rhythm of the pitcher and keep the infielders on edge for bunts and steals. The hit-and-run play is an aspect of aggressive baseball, but it takes polished performers to get away with it. The batter in a hit-and-run play must have excellent bat control, for the pitcher is not likely to hand him a pitch that will be easy to hit into right field, which is where hits, on this play, usually go. The play itself is designed to advance a runner to third from first, when the runner is not adept at stealing. This play is usually called for from the bench by way of the third-base coach. But the hitter and runner must have a sign between them, because complete coordination is required. If the batter forgets to swing, or the runner to run, then the play may foul up completely, even result in a double play. So the aggressive runner, before he gets on base, has reminded himself what the next man's hit-and-run signal is and how he is supposed to respond to it. The man at the plate may give the sign with a special move of his bat or the use of his hands as he picks up dirt or handles the bat between pitches. The runner can acknowledge by kicking the base, adjusting his cap or belt, or in some other manner that cannot be misunderstood.

This play is not a steal, ordinarily, although some managers drop the hit-and-run altogether and make it a steal, with the batter hitting only if the pitch is good. But the standard hit-and-run play calls for the runner to start the moment the pitcher releases the ball. You can't do that on a steal, because you won't have time enough to beat the throw, so you have to take a chance and start when the pitcher goes into his pitching motion. The batter on a hit-and-run is charged with hitting *behind* the runner—that is, hitting the ball into right field, ideally into the spot left vacant as the second baseman moves down to cover the base. A ball hit into right gives the runner a chance to keep on going to third, because he is running away from the ball so that the outfielder has a long throw.

Stengel would not easily forgive a man who got doubled up on a hit-and-run play—that is, was doubled at first on a line drive or a fly ball. He did not see any reason why the runner, busy as he was trying to reach second, could not give a quick glance back toward the plate to make sure the ball was hit safely. A man who has to watch the basepaths as he runs is severely handicapped. Of course, you cannot jog along looking back at the play. You have to put on full speed, but even so you can still take a quick glance, just long enough to assure yourself that the batter has not lined out.

There were other things that would irritate Casey Stengel (or Ralph Houk for that matter), but trying too hard or getting angry at sitting on the bench were not among them. It makes me feel like a traitor to say anything against possessing an indomitable urge to play ball, but I do think that if I had been somewhat less eager to get back into competition, I might have avoided some of the injuries that spoiled so many of my seasons. Sometimes, now that I have my own kids to cope with, I think it is simply a waste of time to give youngsters advice about taking care of injuries and avoiding risks until their hurts have healed. There could never have been anyone more headstrong than myself when I was nineteen and twenty. It would have taken four strong men to keep me from playing basketball or football when I owned not an ache or a pain. So I played, and got hurt, and probably paid for it by losing days and weeks out of almost every baseball season thereafter. The worst of it is that once you have damaged a knee it does not take a severe hurt to put you on the sidelines again. A slight twist, a sudden stop, a quick change of pace or direction, and you feel that stab that means another session on the bench.

Yet you cannot play when you are constantly worrying about a turn or a stop that may lay you up. You have to give baseball all the effort you can spare, or you just won't last in it. So that is one more good reason for listening to coach, trainer, and doctor when they tell you to stay out of competition until the injury is solidly healed. Staying out of competition does not mean staying out of action however. Most physical therapists want a man with an injury, an injured ankle for instance, to move around on it fairly soon, and they always have specific exercises designed to strengthen and repair muscles that have been torn or strained. I was not much of a guy for doing all the exercises that were recommended, but then I guess you can use me for the bad example. I sure did not heal up the way I might have, either, had I performed the isometrics and other exercises as regularly and faithfully as I was supposed to.

I think regularity of exercise is what really counts most. I see some youngsters who think that they can loaf around through all the bad weather and then get into shape by working themselves to the point of exhaustion for a few days. Actually that method is the perfect way to tear or strain a muscle or damage a joint so that you will be on the junk pile for the whole season. There is a common saying in athletics that training does not mean straining. Of course, you have to work muscles out until you feel the bite, but you should condition yourself gradually and take on the tough jobs only when you know you are hardened up enough to handle them. Whether you do pushups or squat-thrusts or straddle-jumps or duckwalks, you start with a few and increase the number gradually. When you hit capacity, you do the same number every day without fail. That is the way to maintain muscle tone so joints will stay in place and bruises will heal up quickly. Take a look sometime over the field of professional athletics and you will find that the coach who is a bug on conditioning and on *full effort* is the one who has fewest athletes laid up with sprains and strains and separations. Of course, there are plenty of injuries like breaks and cuts and contusions that no amount of conditioning can help you avoid. But if your body is in good shape, you can even recover from hard-luck injuries of that sort a whole lot faster than the man who skips the calisthenics.

Notice I say "full effort." It may seem screwy to suggest that that has anything to do with avoiding injury. Yet it does. Severe injuries are sometimes received when a man is relaxed, even goofing off, not ready for the sudden strain or shock that would never damage a muscle that was taut and ready.

A lot of strains and sprains are gathered by players who forget to warm up. Some fellows think that if the day is warm, there is no need to get any warmer. But you can pull a muscle just as quickly in August as you can in March, and it should be part of your routine, no matter how strong and ready you feel, to go through the standard warmup before you play—tossing the ball back and forth, stretching the legs at an easy pace, swinging a bat, bending the knees and back.

Conditioning, of course, includes getting a full share of sleep and taking plenty of care with your diet. I am not going to set myself up as an example in this department. But I am going to point to two of my teammates who have had great luck in avoiding injury, and who have already lasted a long time in baseball and undoubtedly have a good many seasons to go. The most obvious one is Frank Crosetti. Frank is getting close to sixty. But get out there on the diamond and work out with him and see who gets winded first. In an old-timer's game they would have to put chains on Cro to give the others an even chance. No matter what the weather, or where we are, the first man up and out is always Frank Crosetti. He believes in long walks, in early bedtime, and in early rising. He has a lot of ideas of his own about diets, but you never see him stow away an oversize meal, even at a celebration. He eats plenty of fruit, practically never takes a drink, and goes especially light on lunch.

If Frank is the first one up, then Ellie Howard is the second, and Ellie has never had but one or two injuries in his whole career. Ellie too likes to walk, loves to be outdoors, and keeps a close check on his weight at all times. He is strictly a one-cocktail man, gets to bed early, and rises with the chickens, or with Frank Crosetti. Sometimes on the road these two birds will have been up and finished with a mile walk while the rest of us are still trying to order breakfast.

I feel a little foolish to be giving advice about avoiding injury or taking care not to put too much strain on an already injured joint, because I have a long history of injuring myself through failure to avoid unnecessary strains. One winter I put myself out of action just by playing touch football with my son and two brothers. But we just love this game—just as I love regulation football—and I never can stay away from it, even when I know better. As a matter of fact, I think if a man really has the sort of drive you need to be a professional athlete, then it is almost impossible for him to lie around and grow fat in the off-seasons, or even on off-days. The competitive urge is built right into such a person and he has to satisfy it some way. So in November 1964, when I knew better—having put many days and even weeks in on the sidelines because of different injuries—I played touch football in my yard and wrenched my shoulder when trying to make a tag. But that isn't the worst thing I ever did. Late in the 1966 season, when I was just beginning to feel sharp and strong again and starting to hit well, I got into a stupid wrestling match on the road and wrenched one hand so that it swelled up and I could not hold a bat. That is why I say I am probably better as a bad example than as an adviser on this question. But I do know that when you like to compete, you are going to compete, no matter what. And if you play to win, you can't keep fretting over what you may do to a knee or an arm. You can, however, learn a lesson from me and try to avoid taking the foolish chances.

chapter four

When I was still brand new with the Yankees, still convinced my $9,500 salary rated me close to Rockefeller, still trying to get adjusted to my luxurious quarters at the Concourse Plaza Hotel, I had a caller who you might say gave me a glimpse of a future studded with diamonds and lined with gold. He called me so early one morning that he got me even before I had breakfast and begged to talk to me. He said he was a show-business agent who had some very lucrative propositions to discuss. So I saw him, with my face still fresh from the washbasin, and tried to listen without a show of excitement as he talked to me of millions to be made through endorsements and personal appearances. If you can imagine a skinny Steve Allen, with a mustache—heavy black-rimmed glasses, sharply creased clothes, fat-knotted necktie, cufflinks and pinkie ring, then you have a picture of this guy, the first "agent" I had ever known (not counting Frank Scott, who had just started in that business himself and who was more of a baseball type). He talked rapidly and convincingly, lacing all his talk with the names of famous show-business characters and advertising agencies, and identifying everyone, from Dan Topping down, by his first name.

He offered to sign me immediately to a contract that would put me in line to receive my share of the golden flow his other clients were wading in. I knew, as all unsophisticated people knew, that there were uncounted riches in this endorsement business. I also had heard that agents, or personal managers, received half of the total take. At least I knew that's how prizefighters divided their income. So I could hardly wait to sign up for my share. But some country caution did warn me that I ought not to put my signature on the paper until I had had at least a word of advice.

We put off the signing then until we could get a lawyer in to verify the legitimacy of the deal and put his blessing on the project. I signed up then and suddenly had a surge of guilt for not having given Frank Scott a chance to match the offer. So I called Frank and had a meal with him and told him what was cooking. He was deeply skeptical.

"You be sure you have a lawyer look at that contract," he told me, "and make sure he approves of the terms."

I didn't tell Frank about the 50 per cent split but I did assure him that a lawyer had gone over the contract word by word and had marked it sound. What I forgot to tell him was that the lawyer was the agent's own lawyer. It did not occur to me then that each man in such a deal needed a lawyer of his own. A lawyer, I thought, was something like a policeman or a judge, who worked for the law and not for some individual, so one should be as good as another.

As it worked out, I never saw ten cents from any deal this "agent" developed, so there was nothing to split anyway. And by the time I had moved downtown, with my new roommates, Johnny Hopp and Hank Bauer, I had sharpened up enough to know that this deal had been a bad move. The agent, it turned out, was an agent for a few show girls, booking them into smalltime clubs throughout the city, and had no access to the sources of the golden flow he had described. At this time I met another agent who had a deal to offer me in black and white, an endorsement for a hosiery company that would pay me several hundred bucks for the mere use of my name. I had already been advised that my "contract" with the first agent had no standing, inasmuch as I was still not of legal age, so I had no hesitance in signing this deal, which gave the new agent (who later grew famous in another line) something like 20 per cent of the income. It was a legitimate deal all right, agreed to by the company in question. The only trouble is that I never saw any of the money. After that I went back to Frank Scott and asked him to straighten me out. He worked for 10 per cent and he began to make money for me immediately.

Actually it had not been entirely the money that tempted me into these deals. It was the feeling that I was moving into the glittering world I had read about, where famous people called each other by their first names, and nobody ever wanted for anything. What small-town boy could have resisted such an opportunity?

This business of endorsements and personal appearances is a strange one and it took me a long time to get adjusted to the manner in which my market value ballooned within a year. At the start, I recall that I was paid $500 for showing up someplace and signing autographs and looking pleasant. It was hardly more than a year later that Frank got me a $5,000 fee for making an appearance at an outing of some kind—at Bear Mountain or some such place—with all my cash expenses paid in addition. It was not that my doings on the diamond meanwhile were all that spectacular. It was just that what I did accomplish always made the writers envision still greater accomplishments to come, until I would be on a par with the great Yankees of earlier days. Being a Yankee, of course, was a large part of it, and I always felt that the other guys on the club, who had made the Yanks the champions as well as the biggest gate attraction in the league, ought to share somehow in this bonanza that I stumbled on. If I had played in some other city, if Runt Marr had come back with an offer, or if the Red Sox had signed me as they once considered doing, these extra sources of income would not have been open to me, at least not in the same degree. I wasn't leading the league in anything except errors, even though I did get named in

1952 to the All Star team. So most of my market value was based on promise and on just being a Yankee. This is one reason why young players still want most to play in New York.

Actually, in 1952 I missed twelve games because of that twist I gave my knee playing basketball, and that winter I had to have an operation on it. The bone infection (osteomyelitis) that I had carried from my football days had been slowed down by penicillin, so I really would have been sound of limb if it had not been for that knee. I could still run as fast as ever and I was still taking chances in the outfield—something I had to give up on finally, lest a shoestring dive and catch be my last.

It just seemed that every season when I would begin to get some momentum, there would be a twist or a tear or some ailment that required another visit to the surgeon. In 1953 I was out of twenty-four games because of that knee operation. About the only thing I never got was a baseball in the skull. Pitchers never threw close to my head anyway. They soon learned that the one way to make me jump and keep me from digging in was to brush my legs back. A baseball on those ailing gams could really hurt, and might put me on the bench. It was a brutal business I suppose, but I never got sore about it. A pitcher always tells himself you are trying to take the bread out of his babies' mouths when you hit against him, and he uses any legitimate trick he can think of to keep you from getting a toe hold and teeing off on him.

To make up for the series I missed out on in 1951, there were World Series in 1952 and 1953, in both of which I felt strong and hit hard and ran at my top speed. The biggest kick, of course, was my grand-slam home run in Ebbets Field in 1953. Having missed so many games that year because of the operation, and having dropped below .300 in my batting average, I got a special kick out of helping the club take the winner's share in that Series. And I think it may have been that year that I discovered something that was borne in on me again years later—that you really don't put out your best effort unless there is some pressure on you. If your club is out of the running, you may *think* you are spending every last shred of your ability. But you do not really do so—do not dig deep down into those untapped reserves and bring up that final ounce of speed or skill or strength that it takes to nose out the opposition. That is what is so great about competitive sports and what makes them different from the contemplative sports like fishing or hiking. Only when the competition is hot do you really discover what your body can accomplish, and only then do you taste the really sweet satisfaction that comes with winning a prize you thought was out of reach.

In general, the World Series has been a jinx to me, for I always seem to come up with a new injury or have to sit down because of an old one. In 1952 and 1953, however, I played in all the games and helped score plenty of runs.

In 1955 a new pitcher joined the Yankees who worked with me to outwit the opposition pitchers and to help me fatten my average up to where I felt it always should have been. This was Bob Turley, who was, without doubt, the best and quickest reader of pitchers I ever knew. Bob could study a game on television and come up with the little telltale sign that would indicate when a pitcher was going to let go with his fast ball. There was one pitcher, for instance, who would bring his two hands up over his head before throwing the fast ball, but would raise them only nose high before throwing the curve. Another would hold the ball so the seam was showing when he was going to let the fast ball go. Another one always looked down into his glove before the curve. Bob had these and a dozen other tip-offs stored in his head and he would keep his eyes glued to the pitcher.

Not all the batters wanted to be tipped off about pitches. I knew Bill Skowron did better when he was on his own. Although I hit my World Series grand slam off a slow curve, I doted on fast balls and it gave me a good head start to know for sure a fast ball was coming, so Bob would always let go with a piercing whistle when he picked up the fast ball sign. More than once I was able to unload on a pitch because of this advance signal.

There were a few pitchers whose giveaway signs I could pick up myself, after Bob pointed them out to me. One big guy in Boston used to come down so hard on his front foot, when he threw the fast ball, that you could hear the *pow!* and that was as good as a loud whistle to me. Of course, not all pitchers tip off their pitches, and even when I knew what was coming, I did not always tee off on it successfully. As a matter of fact, I was making new marks in strike-outs, leading the league in that department in 1952 and 1954. But I was striking out because I was almost always going for the seats and was not pushing or poking the ball to pile up singles. When you let fly at a ball with all your strength, you increase your chances of missing it. And while I did try to cut down on my strike-outs by staying away from the stuff I knew I could not hit, I did not let them fret me too much, as long as the wallops kept coming.

No doubt about it, 1956 was my biggest year. This year I stayed relatively healthy, with nothing but a slightly sprained knee to slow me down. I believe I missed only four games that season and I had the pitchers pretty well sized up. After I got up a head of steam and began to do well in hits and RBIs as well as homers, I began to yearn after that triple crown—top batting average, most homers, and most RBIs. The writers made much of the fact that I was running right along with Babe Ruth's record in home runs, and I even got into September a little ahead of him. But I honestly never had either hope or ambition about that. I was no Babe Ruth and did not mean to be.

But I sure did want to beat out Al Kaline and Ted Williams and I stayed up to date on what they were doing that season. Of course, I never did catch Babe Ruth, because it takes a lot of mighty blows in September to touch that record. But I had 52 home runs, enough to lead the league, and I had my best big league average yet: .353, with 130 runs batted in. For the first time I felt as if I was really earning all I was being paid, and a little more.

I know there are plenty of guys who come into baseball with a definite idea of how much they are worth and they set right out to get it. I was not that way, for I was grateful to get what I did at the start, knowing it was well above the minimum, and many times what I had ever earned before. But as my market value became clear to me through the endorsement offers I received, I was determined to get what I could while I lasted. It was obvious that my ailments were not going to be wished away, and the fact that my father and his brothers all died young gave me the conviction that I would probably not live to be an old man. All I knew how to do was play baseball, so if I was going to leave my family secure, I had to get as high a price for my services as I could.

The trouble was that I was not much of a negotiator. About all I knew how to do was set a price and then stick to it, trying to avoid being drawn into an argument that could lead to my giving in on the salary. I have to confess that George Weiss had almost always seemed distant and cold to me and immovable as a wall of the Stadium. When I was older, I realized that he was just doing his job—saving as much of the boss's money as he could and trying to leave a little leeway for further raises. But in baseball, especially when an injury is likely to mean the end of your employment, you can't count too much on futures. I was the mainstay of the Mantle family, after my father's death, and I was determined to keep them in comfort. Salaries that sounded big to people outside of baseball could sound pretty ordinary when divided by the number of years I might have to go without any baseball salary at all. So I used to go into those spring sessions determined to bring out all I could.

George Weiss was too tough for me generally, however, and I always had to settle for a number of few pegs below what I had aimed at. But eventually I learned to aim higher than I hoped to get and then I began to wind up with the salary I had in mind. The outside income kept increasing until it actually exceeded what I earned at the ball park. Then I knew something drastic had to be done to boost my salary into the same bracket with other stars.

After taking that triple crown, I lost almost the last vestiges of my uneasiness and found I could open up a little with the writers and not be afraid of saying something foolish, or of not being able to say anything at all.

As a matter of fact, I started off that season feeling more confident in every way. I became a little cooler at the plate, able to adjust to the inside pitches and actually cream them now and then, able to slice the outside pitches and not miss them from trying to overpower them completely, able to let the not-quite-good-enough pitches go by. I was still swinging for distance rather than for average. But I had a far better idea of what I could and could not accomplish.

In my fielding too I found added confidence. I knew there was more to the job than just catching the ball and banging it in. I learned to wait for a base-runner to commit himself and then hang him up with a hard throw. I had learned to keep my eye on the ball that went over my head and to judge the drives that came straight at me. Center field was home to me. I enjoyed the extra range it gave me and I was glad to get away from the sudden stops that right field required. And I had learned to let my throws go with power and style, putting back, leg, and shoulder into them, with lots of confidence that they would hit the target.

I carried that confidence with me into salary negotiations. I had been making $20,000 in 1955 and this was boosted to $30,000. Now I thought the time was ripe to make the big leap. For 1957, having been voted MVP and feeling that I would never be able to make a stronger pitch, I wanted $60,000. So I asked for $65,000. I met with Mr. Weiss in New York in January, after I had turned down their offer of $42,000. There was not much argument on my part, I just listened to what they said and repeated my determination to play for no less than $65,000. Maybe if I had been able to put into words all my reasons for wanting to cash in while I could, the discussion would have been briefer. But I was always tongue-tied in those meetings and never was able to come up with the right phrases until long after the meetings were over. But this time I had promised myself I was not going to budge. Enough of my new confidence carried over to enable me to stick to this resolve. Mr. Weiss raised the offer first to $50,000 and then to $55,000, which was to be "final."

A couple of years earlier I would not have had the courage to hold out past that point. But I just shook my head and stayed put. Then, in the old Yankee style, the problem was laid in the lap of the boss, Dan Topping. Dan thought it over briefly and said, "Sixty thousand, and that's *absolutely* final." And that was what I wanted too, so I signed. And all I wished, after that was done, and I should have felt dizzy with joy, was that my poor father had been allowed to live to share some of the comfort this money could bring. It was his sacrifice, and his dream, and his drive that had put me in the way to make this kind of money, and he was not even to know about it.

Next season I came up with a brand-new ailment—shin splints—really muscle strains in the lower part of my legs. The doctor said they came from playing basketball. But a winter without playing basketball for me would have been like a winter in jail. As a matter of fact, there had been so many banquets and personal appearances and awards that winter, that I think the real trouble was that I played basketball without getting into condition for it. But if I hadn't played something, I'd have probably blown up to 225 pounds with all the rich food and idleness. So I had to settle for shin splints that tortured me when the ground grew hard. In September they pained me most of the time, whether I was running or sitting still. One time they actually cramped my leg so that I had to be carried out of a car into a restaurant. The doctors said that only continual hard running had caused them and that only complete rest would cure them. I took ten days off. But how could I rest when the club was in a scramble for the pennant? I actually felt guilty to be sitting idle on top of my fat salary while the other guys were out there busting their guts. So I got myself taped up and did my best.

In the World Series that season I ran into the jinx again. This was in the third game, when I was on second base. Bob Buhl was pitching and I had a real good lead when Buhl turned suddenly and threw to Schoendienst to pick me off. I lunged head first for the bag and got my right hand on it. The throw was wild. Schoendienst dived for it but missed and he came down with his full weight on my right shoulder.

It was as if someone had dropped a barrel of flour on me and the wonder is that no bone cracked. My shoulder began to ache like a tooth by next inning. I was able to stay in the game, however, and batting left-handed, got another single and a home run.

The shoulder really stiffened up that night, so that next day I could not even swing a bat. I got into the game as pinch-runner but I was really finished for the Series.

The Yankees lost that Series in seven games and for a while I felt really guilty about having been unable to help save it. The writers, however, named me Most Valuable Player again. The year before I thought I had earned that title. This year I did not think I had. But I was delighted with it anyway, and it helped take out some of the sting of the loss, and some of the ache out of the shoulder.

But that shoulder was to devil me for a long time. After the sharp ache went out of it and the swelling was gone, I felt sure it was going to fade away, or at the most just give a good excuse for dodging some of the duller exhibition games. I was getting devoted to golf now, and the shoulder really did not bother me much when I swung a club that winter.

In Florida the following spring I expected to bring my golf handicap down a few notches. After having had to miss the Series I was in no mood to get into a tussle over salary and I was happy to sign for a $10,000 raise. I was especially pleased that I had signed up early and not waited until I was in Florida, because one day, when I had decided to jake it a little and use my shoulder as an excuse to avoid making the trip to an exhibition game, who should be waiting for me at the eighteenth green on the golf course but George Weiss? He smiled rather coldly at me and I tried hard not to look embarrassed, but I could feel the flush creeping up my neck.

"How's the shoulder?" said Mr. Weiss mildly.

"It's okay for swinging golf clubs," I assured him. "But I can't throw."

All the same, I got out there next day and threw. But I got off to a poor start that year—and I have found that a poor start really handicaps me more than it does some people. I think that's because I still had the habit of getting down on myself when I failed to produce as expected and so began to brood and lose both my confidence and my concentration. Once started on that path, I would need only a minor bad break, a cold, a dumb throw, a strike-out or two, to throw me completely. And, of course, my shoulder kept kicking up, until people began to suggest that I would do better to bat right-handed altogether. That, however, I would not do. I hit altogether differently right-handed. I hit with more strength, and with a more level swing. Left-handed, I uppercut the ball and get my distance that way. I was not going to turn into a half-hitter, after all these years, and after the way my father had devoted himself to making me a switch-hitter.

Actually, I did not wind up with too bad a year, although there was a time when I thought (and everybody seemed to agree) that desperate measures might be required to get me hitting again. I was sore at myself most of the season and even though I wound up with an average better than .300, and got a couple of home runs in the Series, I still felt as if I had fallen short of what I ought to have done.

But I did not feel I had done so badly that I deserved a pay cut. There had been a lot of stuff printed and said about my not giving my best efforts and maybe the management began to believe it. But I knew that, even if I had not produced as I had in the two previous seasons, I had sure given it a try. So I was not going to stand still for a $10,000 pay cut, which was what the new contract offered me. I had moved from Commerce to Dallas, where I had started a business, and had built a bigger home. I was not going to start adjusting the Mantle family to a lower standard—not at this point in my career. Once again it was a matter of hanging tough against George Weiss's slick explanations. Finally, I did wind up with a $2,000 raise. But I had wanted a $15,000 raise, to $85,000, so maybe Mr. Weiss really did outmaneuver me. Still, I do want to say that the Yankee management was, over the years, exceedingly generous with me.

The lessons I learned about myself in the next few years are the ones that are going to last me longest. They'll even help me raise my own boys, I think, or at least they'll help me give them advice, which I hope they'll accept.

The middle fifties were probably my merriest years with the Yankees. My father's death, so long foreseen, saddened me for a long time, but it was not the jolt it might have been, for it was almost a blessed release when it came. But it underlined for me the possibility that my own life might be shortened in the same way, and this subconscious conviction may have prompted me to try to pack as much fun into my life as it would hold.

While I was intent on getting my earnings up to where I might feel reasonably secure about my family's future, I was not about to begin to squirrel money away for an old age that I might never see. I was also blessed with a roommate, Billy Martin, who seemed to be the guy who had invented parties. I had not finished growing up, and Billy, who was three years older, had probably decided he was not going to. Anyway, we undertook to enjoy life together, both on the field and off. Sometimes, when we were working out before a game, I would pull out imaginary arrows and shoot Bill dead on the basepaths, and he would set out to destroy me with imaginary hand grenades. Martin was a pet of Stengel's, so Casey never called us on any of our clowning, perhaps because we were both going pretty good most of the time and perhaps too because we never clowned it up during a game. Well, I should not say never, because once we did put on an act on the bench. And that one time Casey did call us on it.

Casey would always try to soothe me when I blew my top at myself, or would make an effort to steer my tantrum in some other direction. When I kicked the water cooler loose from its casing, he would tell me, "The water cooler didn't strike you out." And one time, when I was especially gloomy over the way I was going, he made me a speech about how baseball should be fun, and that a man who did not get fun out of the game was not going to stay loose and do his best.

Billy and I took the old man up on this and the next time Billy struck out, we began to laugh it up together. "A mile over my head!" Billy yelped, and then we would both pretend to break up over it. We kept this up for some time, with both of us pretending to get great laughs out of the way we slashed at bad pitches. Casey watched us sourly for a time, and then he snarled, "That's enough of that!" It was too. But after that Casey never complained about my taking my strike-outs too seriously.

Looking back on it now, I would say that 1959 was my worst year, as far as performance goes, and probably my worst year as far as attitude goes too. I just could not do anything right, and the harder I tried, the worse I seemed to get. I wish I could lay it all to my injuries, but I can't. I've played most of my professional life with ailments of one sort or another—knees, shoulders, groin muscles, legs—and I've never done as badly as I did in 1959. Actually my record was not bad. Leaving out the poor start I got because of my sore shoulder, it would have been a pretty good one. But what got hold of me was my inability to help the club win ball games. Although I have been conscious many times of a record I was aiming at, in actually playing the game nothing matters to me so much as winning. If I hit two grand-slam home runs and we still lost the ball game, I'd be in the dumps afterward, thinking probably of a home run I might have got, or of a dumb throw I made.

This pressure to do better and better, mostly self-imposed, began to spoil both my concentration and my confidence. I would go to the plate impatient with myself and determined to pull myself and the club out of the downhill slide. Then I would whale away at bad pitches one time. Another time, to make up for it I suppose, I would stand and watch a good pitch go by. As Casey used to remind me, if you take too many good pitches, the pitcher can strike you out with just one pitch. And that's what they began to do to me. Of course, what was happening to the club made a difference too. We were in last place at the end of May and by the middle of June we were only in fifth. While I never felt that it was up to me to carry the team, I was pressing, like a lot of other fellows, to boost the club back where it belonged and this added to my frustration, so that sometimes even my good days failed to cheer me up.

But while I was ready to grant that I was not satisfied with my efforts or with my average that season, I was not prepared for what the management tried to do to me in the wintertime. The first version of my 1960 contract really made me boil—a salary cut of $17,000!

Granting that Mr. Weiss always offered a lot less than he was ready to give, I still did not like what this said about the management's opinion of me. I took it as an insult and I made up my mind that I would not even go to spring training if I did not get the money I wanted. So once more I dug in my heels and just kept saying no. And this time Mr. Weiss would not give either.

It may be that they believed I would not be a holdout. I never wanted to be. It was not my nature to refuse to work when the boss asked me to. I would never ask Casey to bench me, no matter how I hurt. And any time he asked me to play, and no matter where he sent me, I'd obey without complaining. Besides, to duck out of training and sit home while the others were playing ball—well, that was against all my father's training and against the deepest urges in my nature. Baseball was a lot more to me than just a way to make money. It was my whole life.

So finally I gave in about ten days after training started, and flew to Florida, where I engaged in a head-to-head struggle with Mr. Weiss again. As usual I had little to say, beyond a refusal to take any such cut as they suggested. No matter what I was earning in my outside activities—and it was not as much as everybody thought—I did not intend to be humiliated in this way, or set back to where I had been three years before. The whole idea bugged me worse than anything that had ever been done to me. Even after they reduced the cut by $10,000 and cut me "only" $7,000, I was still sore about it and had a hard time looking pleasant as I suited up for my first workout. But I felt good and I was determined to put in a real good season again that would make it impossible for them to refuse me a fat raise. Since that day, I have never had the least cause for complaint at the way the Yankees treated me.

But the slump that I had got into the previous season still held me fast. The rest of the club too seemed bent on repeating the previous season, so there was pressure from all sides. Even the fans got on me harder than ever, until one day they got so frenzied they actually jumped on the field and took swings at me. One kid belted me hard enough to give me a sore jaw that lasted almost a week. Well, I was in a mood to belt myself, for I sure was playing like a man who deserved a pay cut.

Once again my concern with how I was going began to spoil my concentration, until I would actually goof off after a failure and forget what was going on on the diamond. I walked away from a third strike and never noticed that the ball had got by the catcher. A few seasons earlier I'd have been off to first like a panther, and might have made it. This time I was halfway to the bench before I saw what had happened, and I hadn't a chance to reach first.

Then, later in the season I did something that my own

father would have benched me for. I actually lost track of the outs, so concerned had I become with my own failures. With Roger Maris on base ahead of me, I bounced a ground ball for an easy force. Thinking there were two out, and disgusted with myself for failing to drive Roger around, I stomped to the bench without running the ball out. It was an easy double play and Stengel blew his stack.

I don't blame him. Nor do I blame the fans for the howls of anger and derision that poured down around me. I hated myself at that moment worse than they did. Casey took me right out of the ball game and told the writers after the game that it was for not running. And what hurt me most, I think, was that Roger had nearly wrecked himself trying to break up the double play—when I wasn't even trying. Of course, I knew I hadn't been loafing. I had just, like a dumb cluck, forgotten the outs. But I felt that I was in disgrace, not only with the fans and with Stengel, but with my teammates.

I found out the next day that I was wrong about my teammates. They were 100 per cent for me, and nearly all of them, cheerfully lying, told me they had often made the same mistake. Well, maybe some of them had. But there were one or two of these guys who had never done any such thing, and I'd have bet my salary on it. But it made me feel good to have them pretend they had. And it also, all of a sudden, made me see things in a very different light. I realized that I had been so concerned with how *I* was doing that I had forgotten about the rest of the club. And that was, by way of thinking, one of the worst sins I could have committed. From now on, I told myself, I was going to put out 100 per cent *all* the time, even if there *were* two outs, and no matter how badly I was doing. It was one thing to punish myself, it was quite another to hurt the club. What's more, it was childish. And, at the age of twenty-eight, I was not a child anymore.

It makes a nice story to imagine that this was one of those "turning points" that saved my whole career. In a small way it was, for it did at least mark my first serious effort to change my attitude. But the change did not come overnight. Indeed, I am still working on it, trying to rid myself finally of kicking the water coolers and putting on the sulks when I miss one. But I knew, and my friends made it clear that they knew, that I was not just putting on an act or looking for sympathy. I just wanted so damn much to win that I could not stand to fail. I was a sore loser and I don't think there's anything really sinful about that—as long as you control its expression.

After that episode I started to come to life at the plate. But I had more going for me than just a change in attitude. I had Roger Maris hitting in front of me, so the pitchers were not "pitching around" me—throwing me nothing but bad pitches and chancing a base on balls—the way they used to. Too often big Roger was there on first base ahead of me, and no pitcher wanted to push him to second base without charge.

The next game after Casey yanked me was a night game with Baltimore, who shared first place with the White Sox at the time. Man, how I wanted to have a good game that night! And how the fans gave it to me when I took my position in center field. But I just closed my ears to everything, even to the catcalls that hailed me when I lined out my first time up. On my second trip, batting left-handed, I really tied into one and rocketed it into the bull pen. I can't describe the wonderful release that gave me. It's one of the extra dividends of baseball, this chance to wallop all your frustrations right square in the nose and drive them out of sight.

I had two more trips to the plate. I flied out to right field next time up and then, with the winning run on base in the last of the ninth, and that old knuckle-ball demon, Hoyt Wilhelm, pitching, I popped a high foul behind the place that should have finished me. But the ball dribbled out of that big manhole cover Clint Courtney used for a knuckle-ball glove and I had one more chance. Hoyt tossed me one more butterfly and this one I had timed just right. It landed in the seats and won the ball game.

Beginning right there we just took off on a streak that led us straight to the pennant, so my getting yanked was a turning point for everyone, even for Old Casey, who was, unbeknownst to everyone except the top brass, completing his final season with the Yankees.

This season, 1960, was just about my healthiest. I don't believe I missed more than one ball game, although I did have aches and pains and sore spots. But so did a lot of others, and nobody let down. We did not even let down in the Series—the only World Series that we lost when we should have won. A wild bounce of a ground ball that hit Tony Kubek in the neck—and a wonderful clutch home run by Bill Mazeroski—beat us in the final game. And good season or no—and I had one of my best—I felt so low after the Series was over that I could hardly peel off my uniform.

I am not going to say I was glad to see Casey Stengel leave the Yankees. Casey had been good to me from the start. It was he who brought me to the Yankees at least a year, and maybe two years, before the upstairs management thought I was ready, and so it was Casey who helped my father realize his dream before he died. Casey taught me a great deal about baseball and helped me through some of my worst spots. He was a smart manager and a good teacher. His patience with me was practically endless. I got sore at him a number of times, as any good ballplayer gets sore at any good manager. But it really saddened me to see him go and I will always count him as one of my best friends.

Still, I was delighted to have Ralph Houk for a boss. Ralph was another man like Harry Craft—a man you could respect, a man who made you want to win for him, and a fellow who hated to lose just as much as I did. When I heard that Ralph was going to move up to succeed Casey, I telephoned him right away to say how glad I was. And when the season began, Ralph did something for me that I think may have added years to my playing career. I know it greatly improved my performance.

What Ralph did was call me the team leader and give me the responsibility of keeping the fight in the ball club, by my own actions and example. This suddenly took me out of myself and made me see that other people had problems and emotions. It just about put an end to my worst sulks and tantrums. I knew I was supposed to be setting the example! Like the officer who can't show how scared he is, lest the soldiers in his command be infected by his fears, I had to fight down my own frustrations and concentrate on winning, so that the younger fellows would learn to do the same.

In performing this job, Roger Maris helped me in an unexpected way. He gave me some head-to-head competition at the plate, by staying either right at my heels or a jump ahead of me in homers. And he took much of the heat off me during the ball games, for he became the favorite target of the Stadium boo contingent. Of course, I still got my share of hoots and boos when I came to the plate. But it was surprising how much more easily I could bear them after telling Roger not to take them to heart. Roger did take it hard after a while, in spite of my sage counseling. But I think I helped him take a philosophical attitude part of the time. And I know I learned to set him a good example.

This new maturity came not just with being almost thirty, but with being made into the club leader. My rivalry with Roger was strong that year. But it never grew personal and never bitter. Roger and I lived together by choice and he was good for me in a lot of ways. He ribbed me, half seriously, about how he was going to beat me out and this kept me on my toes. And he devoted himself to the job with all the intensity of a Hank Bauer. Billy Martin had been an all-out player himself. But when the game was over, and especially if there was a victory to celebrate, Billy could be just as intense about celebrating and I used to try sometimes to stay up to him. Roger, however, was sober, early-to-bed, and single-minded about staying in shape and getting his job done. He was also a tremendous fielder and he took a lot of the pressure off me in the outfield, for he could range far and fast.

But being made into the take-charge guy is what did the most to change my attitude on the playing field. I just could not let Ralph down, no matter how strong was my urge to blow my top at a strike-out or an error. Ralph saw to it that I got the salary I wanted—$75,000, the most I had ever made—and he gave me a lot of sound specific advice, about trying to cut down on my swing to reduce my strike-outs, for one thing. And he left it up to me to decide when I was too hurt to play—or at least, he never failed to check my condition and ask me if I felt up to playing. Casey usually left it to me to ask to be taken out and it just is not my nature to beg off my job when the pennant race is on, if I can in any way drag myself to the plate.

I kept on having ailments of one sort and another. But some of them were trifling and some of them were my own fault for doing something stupid. I actually wrenched a muscle in my neck once just from being so damn angry at striking out. I had got back to the bench, after Dave Moorehead had struck me out for the fourth time in a row. I put the stupid bat in the rack, and could not let go of it without expressing my anger. So I tried to snap the handle of the thing by arm pressure, and gave myself a bad neck. Can you imagine my asking to be excused from play for that? I would go to the plate with my head askew first.

As a matter of fact, if Ralph Houk had asked me to, I'd have gone to bat with one arm chopped off at the elbow. He was the sort of guy that made you feel he would never ask you to do anything he would not cheerfully do himself. Some managers give you the idea that they are bench representatives of the management, sent to keep you on your toes and keep you trying. But Ralph was always 100 per cent for the ballplayers. When he asked you to do something, you *wanted* to do it, and you tried twice as hard.

Still I would never insist on playing if I thought I could

not produce in some way, or if I thought my being on the field would let the club down, or let Ralph down, which amounted to the same thing. Sometimes I could not run too well or throw with full strength. But as long as I could hit, I knew I could help.

I did not miss many games in 1961, even though I did wrench an arm muscle when swinging the bat left-handed. But I bunted the next time at bat and then I used a heavy bat to keep myself from overswinging (a 36-ounce instead of my usual 33) and actually got a home run that way. There always seems to be some way you can compensate for an ailment or get around it if you really want to play ball, as I always did when the race was hot. Of course, I was getting a fat salary and this, plus my feeling for Ralph, increased my sense of obligation to the club. Besides, there is always added pressure when the club is in the race, and you can often do things you might think you could not do. It really takes pressure to bring out the best in me, or in almost any competitor, I think. Even a runner, racing against time, will not give out the way he will if there is a rival right on his heels.

Later in the season I got myself an infection of some sort that finally did bench me. It may have developed from a cold I picked up, or maybe I was just not getting as much rest as I should and so became easy pickings for a team of microbes. Whatever it was, I developed an abscess on my hip that finally needed surgical treatment to drain it. That really was a mess. But after Dr. Gaynor had cut me open and bandaged me up, I was able to get into the Series. As a matter of fact the doctor would have had to strait-jacket me to keep me out of the Series. When you are going good, baseball is the most exhilarating experience in the world and to be forced to sit and watch it when you should be playing is worse than smelling a sizzling steak just out of reach when you are starving. It isn't any great act of self-sacrifice to get into the game, even when you have a sore tail, as I had. It's just second nature.

I did sit out the first two games of the Series, and that

was all I could stand. I got into the third and fourth games and finally got myself a good solid hit off Jim O'Toole. All I could make out of it was a single, even though it went far enough to be a double. But, just as the doctor warned me, I busted open the incision in the act of walloping the ball and so had to come out. But he had assured me it would not get any worse and I had all winter to heal up, so I did not berate myself in the least. If I hadn't been bleeding, I'd have wanted to keep on playing. And I don't mean that I was trying to be a hero either. I was straining at the leash all the time to get into that Series and the abscess was just a pain in the ——— hip.

Roger beat Babe Ruth's record that year, but the strain really told on him. Toward the end, with fans scratching at him, and writers after him every ten minutes or so for new comments, his hair actually came out in bunches. He was an example to me of what it can do if you let public pressure really get to you and I think trying to buck him up and teach him to take it all a little less seriously actually gave me a new point of view that has made my life easier. I know that since those days I have found it a whole lot simpler to relax in public, and to let the boos bounce off my back. People have said that a teacher often learns more from teaching than the pupil does from being taught. And I guess in a way that in trying to teach Roger to keep his cool, I learned how to keep my own.

But mostly I learned from being given that extra responsibility. Discovering that I was to be the good influence rather than the bad example made me take a new grip on myself and begin to see the world through somebody else's eyes besides my own.

The year of 1962 was the year that my legs really betrayed me. Up to then I could still get off the mark in the old way and turn on the juice when I needed that bit of extra speed. But that year, without any warning, my carved-up right knee suddenly gave way on me. It snapped as I was in the act of sprinting down to first on a drive that the shortstop grabbed on one bounce with a miracle stop. I knew I had that throw beat, because I was really turning it on. Then suddenly the leg went *pop* and the basepath came up to meet me. I went down like a slaughtered steer and I could feel the jolt when I hit the grass. It was like 1951 all over again. The pain practically turned my brain blue. I did not lie still this time, because I was really frantic to get to that base, and I clawed at the ground to pull myself up. As I went down, I felt the stab of pain in my other knee too. I always had an immediate feeling of guilt about getting hurt and I cursed myself desperately for having done it again. This time I wanted no stretcher. I was going to force myself to believe that it was not as bad as it seemed.

It was not so bad either. There was a torn muscle in the right thigh but the left knee was all right. It had just taken a severe wallop when it hit the hard ground with all my weight on it. Altogether I missed almost thirty games. I went home to Dallas to get well but I could not stand being so far from the action and finally I went back to the club, even though I knew I could not move around on the field yet. At least I could get batting practice and not go completely stale. I returned to the line-up after a month and got one of my biggest thrills when I came up as a pinch-hitter in Cleveland. Determined not to strike out, or hit the ball on the ground, when I would have to run, I managed to belt one into the stands to score three runs. The way those fans—Cleveland fans—stood up and roared really took hold of me as no applause ever had before. I could feel the skin getting tight on my neck as I hobbled around the bases. It was like being a kid again and hearing the stands screaming for a run I had made in a football game. Those fans yelled and yelled and kept pounding their hands long after I reached the dugout. It more than made up for every boo or catcall that had ever been thrown at me. I was so choked up over it I could not speak but just grinned foolishly as the guys pounded my back in the dugout. Even now I like to think about that time and hear the noise in my mind again. It's one of the things that makes the game so great.

I did some more pinch-hitting before I got to start a

game again and I believe this pinch-hitting practice helped my hitting, or at least my batting average. I learned to wait for my pitch, coming up all the time with the pressure on the pitcher, and this brought me a lot of bases on balls, and cut down on my strike-outs. The season was a good one for me, in spite of a few more missed games with bumps or bruises of some sort. I discovered I could still run, stole a few bases, and wound up with thirty home runs—no threat to Babe Ruth, but a lot of satisfaction to me. We won the pennant again and met the Giants in the World Series—not a subway Series this time but an airplane Series, with the Giants now 3,000 miles away. We took the Series too, but no thanks to anything I did, because it was one of the worst World Series I ever had, without even a single lonesome run batted in. I played in all seven games too and went to bat twenty-five times. But that National League pitching tied me all up. My best effort was a two-bagger in the second game, in which Jack Sanford shut us out. Outside of the Series, however, it was my best season for getting on base. Every other time I went to bat I made it to first base, or farther. And I credit that largely to Ralph Houk's coaching and to the experience that helped me wait for my pitch. I had only seventy-eight strike-outs in 1962. Two years earlier I had led the league in that category, as I had done several times before. And I got my big thrill in being named Most Valuable Player for the third time in my life.

In 1963 I had one of my real tough years, as far as being laid up is concerned. I got into only sixty-five games, the fewest I had ever played in since I became a Yankee. What laid me up longest was an accident in Baltimore, one that I sometimes tell myself could be blamed on the schedule. Not that I really want to blame anyone. I had hit the top in salary by then and I don't feel that baseball owes me anything, least of all a soft job. But the scheduling has become brutal, and even the younger players feel it now and then. This time we had a night game in Los Angeles on get-off day, followed by a double-header in Baltimore. It was three o'clock in the morning, Los Angeles time, when we left; and we landed at Baltimore at ten in the morning—just about time to get to the park. Everybody was tired for those five games, so tired that it was hard to put any heart into the game. Believe me, late in the second game of the double-header there were not too many Yankees who cared about much more than getting the game over.

In my new role as club leader I really had to reach down into the reserves to find the drive I needed to keep putting out my full effort. I made one desperate run after a fly ball that took me right to the center-field fence, could not stop as I wanted to, and broke my foot against the wall. This took me out of action for another good long time. As usual, in trying to compensate for one injury I put undue strain on another joint and damaged my left knee, making myself eligible for still another operation.

My reason for reciting all these ailments is not to make excuses for my showing, or for my failure to do all the things the sportswriters had promised I could do, but to show how one small injury can lead into a whole flock of others, or how trying to play with an injury that is not quite healed can earn you a number of weaknesses that you might have avoided. Trying to ease up on an injured toe shortened Dizzy Dean's career by forcing him to throw in such an unnatural fashion that he damaged his arm. And getting into the line-up with a limp, or before the last muscle tear was completely healed, gave me two bum knees instead of just one.

The knees, however, could be taken care of, with careful bandaging and support—and an effort to avoid the sudden stops and turns and tumbles that outfield play can lead you into. I learned how to bandage my legs so the knees could hold up through a game. There was some pain, especially in the late innings, but it was not unbearable and not any more than a lot of other fellows have put up with. I could run and slide, and best of all I could stand at the plate and take my cuts either right-handed or left. I was well enough to get into the World Series in 1963 and at least make an effort to help save our hides.

But who could beat Koufax and Drysdale that year? In that Series, they were the best pitchers I had ever seen; and I counted myself lucky to get a home run off Sandy and a single off Drysdale, to give me a batting average for the Series that was about the size of my little boy's collar. This was the worst beating I had ever seen the Yankees take and it left me aching for another crack at this club. But that was not to be, and may never be. At least we'll never have to face Sandy Koufax again, and that may be a good thing for everybody's batting average.

Although the operation on the left knee hobbled me some in 1964, I managed to get into all but nineteen games, the best I'd done since 1961. Roger Maris, who had been laid up a good part of the previous year too, was playing full time again, and again was making my lot much easier to bear—getting all the grief from the outfield fans and also keeping the pitchers honest. As a matter of fact, the whole club looked good that season, which was Yogi Berra's first as manager. Yogi had long been a pal of mine, one of those fellows who just makes you feel good all over when you see him. People were saying he would not be able to hold the club in line the way Ralph had. Well, Yogi certainly was not Ralph and did not pretend to be. No one, in my book, could ever match Ralph Houk. But I know I was just as eager and just as ready to take my orders from Yogi as from any manager I had ever had. I had no ambitions to run the club and never expect to have any. It is my nature to play wherever and whenever the manager says, without beefing. Running a baseball club takes a whole lot more than an ability to play baseball on big league level. That's why I don't believe I'll ever be a manager. Whatever that extra something is that some guys have—and sometimes guys have it who have not been especially outstanding as players—I don't think it's part of my make-up.

My skills all came to me naturally, through steady practice and a love of the game, and I doubt if I could ever develop that shrewdness and tenacious memory that Casey Stengel had, for instance, or his patience at correcting mistakes for the younger players. I am sure I could never find Ralph Houk's secret for instilling a fighting spirit in a club, or share his gift for winning the respect and devotion of the ballplayers. Nor do I think I could ever store up in my head all the baseball knowledge Yogi Berra has gathered, the strengths and weaknesses of pitchers, the habits of hitters, the tactical possibilities of every situation.

People always liked to make jokes about Yogi's mental ability. But actually he was one of the fastest thinkers I ever saw. One day he saved a ball game by some rapid thinking and fast action that half the people who saw it did not even understand. He was on third base with one out, and the infield drawn in to cut off the run. The batter (I don't recall who) bounced a ball to the shortstop and Yogi put his head down and gave a tremendous imitation of a man trying to score. The shortstop, after a split second's hesitation, banged the ball home. But by the time he had let go of the ball, Yogi had already slammed on the brakes and was scrambling back to third. When the catcher got the ball, it was too late to get the man at first, and there was no play on Yogi either. That fake had saved us an out and so gave us still another chance to score Yogi with a sacrifice. It was split-second thinking and split-second timing.

Yogi always surprised people with his speed on the basepaths anyway. He seemed built to be slow, with those heavy, awkward-looking legs, and the knock-knees. But he had been a soccer player as a kid and really could get over the ground in a hurry.

We had to scramble for the pennant in 1964, and so did the Cardinals. As a matter of fact there was a time late in the season when it seemed a pretty sure bet that neither of us would make it and that the Series would be played in Chicago or Philadelphia. But everybody stayed well and we had our share of luck too. We didn't know it, but it was the last time around for several of us and the last time we'd even be in contention for a long while. Our pitchers looked great, especially Bouton and Stottlemyre, and there was no reason to suppose that they would not put in many more strong seasons.

The Series for me was one of severe ups and downs. My ability in the outfield was not what it had been and in the fifth inning of the third game I let a ball get away from me that cost us the tying run. Errors never made me feel especially cheerful. But this one, which looked, from the way the Cards were going, as if it would cost us the game, really stung me. Happily, I had outgrown the stage of hanging my head and forgetting the rest of the ball game. Instead I just went up to that plate with a determination to demolish the first good pitch they gave me. My chance came in the last of the ninth. I was first up that inning, and the pitcher was Barney Schultz, one of those knuckle-ballers that can drive you out of your mind. When they break off that flutter-ball, not even the catcher can follow it, and the batter is lucky to get even a small piece of it. But the first knuckler Barney threw did not break at all. It just hung up there, big as a basketball, looking like one of those pitches my father would toss me when I was eight years old. I needed just one look at it and then I cut loose with the full power of the bat. It went right out of the park and won us the ball game.

When I came across the plate, the whole club was waiting for me and I really thought they might cripple me up for the rest of the Series with the pounding they gave me on the shoulders and back and the way some of those gorillas threw bear hugs on me. They were no happier than I was about it, for I felt it had wiped out the error I made. If we had not won that game, I know I'd have carried that defeat around with me for months and it would have tortured me like a boil. It turned out that that blow was my sixteenth in World Series competition and put me one up on Babe Ruth for World Series homers. But that really was not of first importance to me. It remains one of the few home runs I remember vividly, not because it broke a record, but because it won a game I thought I had lost.

In 1965 I began to feel that I was truly headed downhill

and I took a lot of the blame for it on myself. My shoulder, which I thought had pretty well healed, began to bother me more and more, and no amount of treatment seemed to ease it. It took me a time to admit it to myself, but I just couldn't uncork those long throws any more—and I used to love to bang that ball in from the deep outfield. Casey had worked on me to use the full strength of my arm that way and he used to urge me to let fly with my whole body, letting my hind foot come right up off the ground in my follow-through. It was nearly as much fun as swinging the full length of the bat at a good pitch. Both the full swing and the full throw were efforts I just could not hold back from. Part of the time I did cut down on my swing a little but every so often I had to cut loose, even if the follow-through put me on my knees. And the same way with my throw. Despite any small twinge in my shoulder, I just had to power that ball in across the diamond when there was a need for it.

As the 1965 season grew older, however, I just could not throw the ball the way I used to, nor could I charge a ball and make a sudden stop in my old style, what with both knees threatening to kick back on me. Most of my career, and certainly in the early years, my speed and my throw could compensate for my occasional misjudging of a ball, particularly a drive that came right to me. Nowadays, having lost part of my speed, I give away a step to the runner when I go after a ball in the outfield, and the opposition, knowing this, were able to take more chances with me. But when my arm went too, I began to look something like a dead weight on the outfield. It is true I could judge a ball a lot better, and could nail flies that I might have had to give up on when I was playing them improperly. But finally I had to have help with every throw. Indeed, I never threw the ball back to the infield at all, but would flip it to Tom Tresh and let him fire it in.

As long as I was carrying my weight at the plate, I did not let this fret me too much. But my wobbly pins, especially my right knee, made it more and more difficult for me to deliver a long blow. My average stayed up pretty well but the home run production and the runs batted in really tumbled, down below what I had done in my first year as a Yankee. My nineteen home runs were the least I had ever collected, except for the year when I appeared in only sixty-five games. Even that year I managed fifteen homers and thirty-five runs batted in. But 1965 was certainly my low point, and not from want of trying. It is true that the rest of the club was having its troubles, with Maris out of the game a good part of the year and Ellie Howard suffering from a bad arm, so we very soon found ourselves fighting just to stay in the first division.

I had got off to a bad start that year in a game against Kansas City when I slid too late and hit the bag hard. One leg went all the way over the base and the other slammed against it, starting me on a round of limping again. Then, in June, against Kansas City again, I was straining to score from third on a passed ball and would have made it too, but three strides from the plate I tore a hamstring muscle and could hardly hobble in. I healed up enough to get back into the line-up. But altogether that year I missed forty games. It was generally a jinx year for the club, with so many injuries knocking holes in the line-up and poor Johnny Keane, our new manager, was nearly out of his mind trying to patch a workable combination together.

I could not blame my own showing on the way the club was performing, however. Instead I felt that it was up to me to lead the way. But I had to face the fact that it was physically impossible for me to do so. That shoulder was not a sprain or a tear. Instead there was something in there that drove knives into me whenever I threw and that lamed the muscle so I could hardly use it. And the bum knee made it difficult for me to get full leverage into my swing, especially when I batted left-handed. As usual, there were people who suggested that I would do better to bat right-handed all the time. Perhaps if I had been playing Boston or Washington, where the left field fences are right handy, I might have listened to that advice at last, to close out my career as a right-handed hitter. But in Yankee Stadium the short fence is in right field and my left-handed uppercutting swing was made to order for the home park.

Anyway, while I was not delivering those long blows, I was hitting fairly well and I felt that a winter's rest and some treatment would get me off to a good start again. That fall, however, I really did a job for myself, and in typical fashion. I have always been active in the off-seasons, playing golf whenever the chance offered and hunting or fishing in between times. Golf is my real addiction, next to baseball, not to watch, but to play. But I just can't consign myself to slouching in front of the TV in my off-time. And with a family of active boys I have to be up and moving around a good part of the time. The family sport is touch football. I'd play real football if I could, because I really am devoted to that game and just eat it up during the season. But touch football, the way we play it, is rough enough—too rough, as it turned out.

We were playing in our yard, sometime in November—my brothers Ray and Butch against Mickey, Jr., and me. The game grew hot and I got completely immersed in it, so that when Butch dodged by me with the ball I made a wild lunge, bad shoulder or no, and put the tag on him. Man, that shoulder really hurt. I knew without being told that I had wrecked it. For a long time it was just no use to me at all and I could see I was going to be completely helpless in the field and at bat. The winter grew longer and I tested it out a few times. But it was obviously not going to be better. In fairness to Ralph Houk, I knew I would have to tell the Yankees that I was not going to be able to play again. I telephoned Ralph but he just would not take what I said as final. Eventually I made a trip to New York to see him, and I brought with me the man who was head of the insurance company I had just bought into. I knew he could explain to Ralph better than I could just what my plans were for the future and why I could not ever play ball again.

Ralph listened to it all sympathetically and then asked me as a favor just to have the shoulder looked at in the hope that an operation might make it well. It felt to me as if nothing short of amputation would ever relieve it, but I could not refuse Ralph's request. So I went out to the Mayo Brothers to let them look at it. I guess it is not hard to imagine some of the fears I had while I was waiting for them to come up with the results, or the relief I felt when they told me that my trouble was simply bone chips and calcium deposits—and curable.

It was a long but not a dangerous operation and it left me with a scar long enough to reach partway to first base. It meant no golf or touch football for a long time, and an even longer wait before I would know if I could throw and swing a bat again.

At least I did not have to worry about my job. Sick or well, I was signed for the Yankees for another season and hoping to be strong as ever. It did not seem possible that Jim Bouton could have another season as bad as the last. Ellie Howard, whose banged-up elbow had been operated on the previous summer, was fully recovered. Roger Maris' pulled muscle and bad hand would probably heal. Al Downing, our hard-working little left-hander, was about due for a big year. And my roomie, Whitey Ford, had made a good recovery from his operation and had helped keep the Yanks from tumbling even further than sixth place. Then we had Mel Stottlemyre, who had been nearly invincible, and he should certainly have been ready for another twenty-game season.

Just what happened to the Yankees, outside of growing old and running into some hard luck at the start, I cannot say. It surely was not the fault of Johnny Keane that we hit the chutes as we did. There was no "revolt" against Johnny, nor any feeling that he did not do his job. It was the players who let Johnny down rather than vice versa and I guess many of us were too involved with our own troubles to be concerned with what it all meant to John. We may have subconsciously felt that Ralph Houk was the real boss and that anybody else was an interloper. But this idea that we would not play for Johnny Keane when we would play for Ralph—well, the answer to that is that, after Ralph came back, we kept right on sliding downhill until we could go no further.

A team collapse of this sort is self-perpetuating. When you know you are out of the race, you just cannot seem to get that extra drop of energy out of yourself that it takes to make the big play. You can tell yourself that you are doing your best. You can even *feel* that you are doing your best and that you could not run any faster, swing any harder, or pitch any more sharply. But without the prod of competition you cannot produce that premium performance. Pressure of competition acts something like fear in that it seems to release some extra juice into your blood stream that makes you do things you are not ordinarily capable of. And the lack of competition, or the feeling of being out of the race, will cause you even to have mental lapses you would not think yourself capable of.

The Yankees, for instance, missed the cut-off man on throws from the outfield so many times that I lost track. We surely lost some of our many one-run losses because of those failures. Turning some of those close ones into victories could have raised us two or three places in the standing. So you see how little it takes sometimes to turn a slump into a disaster. By the same token, it does not take much extra effort, or too many good breaks, to change a seemingly hopeless team into a contender. If the talent is there, you know it is not going to evaporate overnight.

As for me, I managed to pull a hamstring muscle a few times, so that I was something less than a full-time performer. But when I did feel good—and that was more often as the season progressed—I found I still had the same desire, in spite of my advancing years. I still would try a steal if I saw a good chance, even though I knew it was giving Ralph gray hairs to see me run. It was just an irresistible impulse with me. At the plate I still swung both right and left and while I broke no records I did well enough to persuade me that I was still of some use to the club. And as long as I can help us win, I am ready to try. When I feel good, there is nothing I like better to do than play ball. I do not strain on the leash in the spring the way I did when I began, and training often becomes a drag. But once the action begins, I want to be part of it. I can no longer go and get them in the outfield as I could a few years ago and I am not ready to take chances with sudden stops and diving catches. The runners gain a step on me now and I doubt if I ever again get up near twenty in outfield assists. But if I can keep from ruining my shoulder in a touch football game, I know I am still going to be able to hit. And hitting is the way I can help the Yankees most.

LESSON FOUR

Anyone who has ever raised boys into their teens knows what a complete waste of breath and nervous energy it is to try to talk them out of doing the fool things that all boys seem bound to do. It is like trying to talk sense to a drunk. And it is often the same way trying to persuade an athlete to "take care" of himself by not getting into competitive games off-season, by not taking unnecessary chances with a bad knee or shoulder, by getting the sleep he needs, and by trying to keep from adding new lard to his frame. If a man did not have an incurable urge to compete, he would probably not be a professional athlete in the first place. So to ask him to amputate that urge to get into action is asking him to become a non-athlete. And if he does that, he is worse than injured. He is incapacitated. And when a young man feels good, it is not easy to make him believe that an old injury still lurks in some joint to rise up and fell him without warning. Above all, when a man is still young enough to enjoy the good things of life, and has sweated to attain them, it is demanding an acute sacrifice to ask him to forgo them all lest he shorten his career. For all he knows, he may be doomed to a short career anyway.

I think it would help, however, if young fellows who get into organized baseball would stop and take a look at what baseball can do for them—or what they can do for themselves if they make a success in the game. Maybe then they would give more thought to year-round conditioning, to avoidance of useless risks, and to postponing some of the self-indulgence that good pay makes possible. Most ballplayers work hard and stay in good shape while they are hungry. It is success that often causes a man to ease up, just as he reaches his full potential. Sometimes a pitcher will hit the chutes just because he refuses to accept the fact he cannot get batters out in the same old way, because he refuses to develop a new pitch, and refuses to concentrate on his work as men in the serious professions have to. Or an infielder will allow himself to grow fat off-season and be unable to get back to his playing weight in the spring—and will refuse to recognize that he has lost a half-step this way. The good-fellowship of the clubhouse will all seem so hearty, and the hero worship outside the park will grow so fulsome that the ballplayer just cannot believe they will not last forever, or that they are in any way connected with the husbanding of his skills.

It is right to enjoy the game, to stay loose in it, to relax completely off-hours. But in professional sport you just cannot coast, or turn your work into a sideline, with your social life becoming your chief interest. In professional baseball your social life, once your skills begin to diminish ever so little, can take some very strange bounces. You can be the idol of New York swingers one week and next week be looking for a pad in Binghamton, or in Richmond, Virginia.

That's why it helps to stop and count over the rewards available to those who give baseball their best. It can completely change the life of your whole family—move you into a better neighborhood, put your kids through college, provide comforts for your parents, brighten your wife's home and widen her social life, assure you of a head start in some prospering business after you have left the game. But these rewards just don't come incidentally, because you are so popular, or because you have one real good pitch, or because you have an ability to drive inside fast balls a long way. When the batters begin to time your good pitch; when the pitchers start curving you on the outside; when you fall off half a second on the baselines—then your popularity may evaporate like a Florida tan. The people who used to beg you to stand up and sing your favorite ballads, the resort owners who put your whole family on the cuff, while you just signed autographs and played the guitar, the publishers who pestered you to put your by-line on books—they may all be looking the other way now when you go by. You may find that you have no bargaining power left when it comes to talk salary. You may even discover that every club in the league will pass you up.

The men that stay on top in the majors are usually the ones who take a businesslike attitude toward their work. If the pitchers start getting them out, they concentrate on cutting down their strike zone, on avoiding the pitch they have been going out on, on cutting down on their swing so as to drive the outside pitch to left field instead of popping out in a vain attempt to overpower it.

Of if a pitcher who has depended on his strength finds that batters have finally begun to time his hard pitch, while ignoring his curve, he will, if he is a serious professional, not blame the umpires or grouse that the manager is not giving him enough work. Instead he will begin to practice hard to keep that curve in the strike zone, or will develop a new pitch to provide him one more way to upset the batter's timing.

Let me give you some examples. Jim Bunning was once strictly a hard-ball pitcher who depended entirely on his sizzling fast ball to get batters out. When he was with Detroit in the fifties and early sixties, he was as quick a pitcher as you'd want to face. He twice led the league in strike-outs and in 1958 pitched a no-hit, no-run game against the Red Sox. But all that time he really had only two pitches—his fast ball and his curve. And only his fast ball was dependable. He had a change-up of sorts too but could not count on getting it into the strike zone. Now many a pitcher would figure after he had thrown a no-hitter and had led the league in strike-outs he was about as good as anyone. But Jim, who was "real shaken up" after that no-hitter, from the nervous strain of pouring that fast ball through, did not consider himself a complete pitcher by any means. For the next six years, even while he was still posting plenty of strike-outs, he worked to control his curve and change-up, and he started to develop a slider. In 1963, his eighth season with Detroit, he gave up a whole lot of runs and the Detroit management apparently felt he was approaching the end of the road. They traded him right out of the league, to the Philadelphia Phillies. And all Jim did after that was pitch a *perfect* game against the New York Mets. This time he was cool and relaxed. He was finally getting both curve and change-up into the strike zone and had a low slider that really was a killer. He was a complete pitcher finally and his confidence had grown in proportion to his skills. If you have ever seen Jim close up, you would know that he stays in top shape all year round. I doubt if you could get him away from the Phillies for less than a whole ball club, and he looks strong enough to last as long as Warren Spahn.

Or, to get back to my own league, take a look at Gene Woodling. When Gene first came to the big leagues, someone had persuaded him to use an open stance, on the theory that it would enable him to get good wood on every pitch that came into the strike zone, particularly those inside pitches they like to handcuff left-handed batters with. Gene's method worked fine in the minors. He led the Ohio State League with a .398 average his first year up and later on led the Eastern League twice. Then he moved up to Cleveland. He hit pretty well in a very few games before he went into service. When he came back two years later, he hit .188! So back Gene went to the minors, after putting in part of a season with Pittsburgh. It was now eight years since he had started in the game and he did not seem to be moving ahead as he should. But Gene is another fellow who stays in good shape and takes his work seriously. He was lucky enough to land in San Francisco, where Lefty O'Doul told him to get back to a more comfortable stance, no matter how strange it might look. He encouraged Gene to crouch a little to diminish his strike zone. And he let him crowd the plate as close as he pleased, and wind himself right back until he looked at the pitcher over his shoulder. Gene repaid Lefty for his help by belting the ball for an average of .385 to lead the Pacific Coast League. Then he came to the Yankees and has been in the big leagues as outfielder or coach ever since. Had Gene allowed his fat batting averages to persuade him that nobody could teach him anything, he might never have made a comeback. But he was in baseball for a living and he meant to make it a good one.

Gil McDougald is another fellow who was not too proud to make a change in his batting method. Of course, Gil could have held on to many a job with his glove, for he was second baseman number one, when they let him play there. The Yankees had second basemen, however, and they needed Gil at third, so he played third and starred at the job. He also did some mighty hitting. In 1951 he drove in six runs in one inning. But he was really an unusual sight at the plate. He stood with one foot aimed at the third baseman and with the bat drooping over his shoulder as if he were carrying a sack of potatoes on the far end of it. Still, as long as he hit, no one wanted to tamper with that stance. When his hitting started to fall off, however, Casey finally asked him to hold his bat up, in the "cocked" position, so he could swing with less waste motion. Gil followed the advice and immediately improved his average.

Here was an instance where I suppose you might say a man carried the notion of being "comfortable" a little too far. It is right to be comfortable as long as you stay in position to do the job you are up there for. A batting swing, as you may have noticed, starts with a backward motion—a sort of tightening of the spring, or cocking of the gun hammer. Because Gil had his bat drooping behind him, he had to make an extra motion, first to get his bat up, and then to get it back far enough to start his swing. There is also danger, when you try to get too comfortable, of relaxing your grip on the bat. You must take a good tight hold, a really fierce hold on your bat handle, if you want to transfer the full muscle power through your bat to the ball. Some youngsters hit feebly, or foul out a lot, because the pitch actually drives the bat backward when it strikes. The cure for this is a good tight grip—lots of strength in the hands, which you can develop very simply, the way Frank Crosetti does it, by carrying around a small rubber ball and squeezing it constantly.

I might also point out, while we are talking about fellows who improved themselves, that serious athletes are not afraid to listen to advice. A sense of importance that makes a man feel he is too good to accept advice from somebody he considers a has-been, or a never-was, can really bring a baseball career to a sudden close. No one is ever so good that he cannot use advice. Ted Williams, my choice for the finest batter who ever lived, talked batting with everybody who knew anything about the subject. I am not going to say he followed all the advice he got. But at least he listened. There is no telling where the tip may come from that will help you cure a fault.

There was a pitcher in the league not long ago—and I am not going to mention his name—who had one really fine season and decided then that he knew all there was to know about pitching. An old-timer began to advise him not to work so hard to attain perfect control, that he was actually taking off a little zip from his fast ball by trying to pinpoint every pitch. Actually, any good fast ball is going to be alive, and will shoot a little one way or the other as it crosses the plate. So if you get it into the strike zone, it is bound to hit the corners of the plate. But this pitcher would not believe that. He felt it was up to him to stick that ball through tiny holes where the batter could not reach it. So his fast ball lost some speed. And believe me, there is nothing better to hit than a fast ball with just a little speed missing. So pinpoint control did this man no good at all and he soon found himself blowing his top at umpires and sliding very slowly downhill. I have a feeling he will smarten up before it is too late. I hope so, because he still has plenty of natural ability.

Speaking of blowing the top, and speaking as a man who knows how to do just that, I want to add that you cannot become a really serious professional until you learn to avoid these public exhibitions of rage and disgust. Naturally, you will hate to lose, and will be often angered at a poor call or a dumb mistake of your own. But the pitcher who slams his glove on the ground, who kicks the rosin bag into the hereafter, who shakes his fists at the heavens—he is the man the opposition soon gets "on," because there is nothing a hitter likes better than a pitcher who is rattled. And the baseman who, instead of scrambling after a missed throw, pounds his fist on the base or stops to kick dirt—he is the man who may cost his club a run, or give a runner two extra bases.

There is a difference between this sort of showboating and

the reaction of a man who just hates to lose. I think a professional ballplayer ought to be a sore loser. I don't mean a sore loser in the sense that he refuses to exchange a kind word with the winner, and complains that it was somebody else's fault, or hollers that the umpires cheated, or some such thing. I mean a fellow who genuinely hates to lose, who cannot be cheerful in the face of defeat, and who makes up his mind to go out next time and wipe that beating off the books. That is the spirit my father tried to instill in me and which, after some serious effort, I think I acquired.

But that does not mean a player should dwell on his defeats. The worst thing a hitter can do is start brooding over the fact that a certain pitcher *always* gets him out. Instead he should dwell on the fact that he can hit other pitchers just as strong and just as fast as this guy, so there's no reason why he should not find a way to clobber this guy too.

A good hitter puts his strike-outs out of his mind. If a man whiffs you, you do not go up there next time looking to have him fan you again, and afraid to wait for your pitch. Instead you go back determined to knock this guy right off the mound. And that does not mean you become impatient and take a cut at the first thing that comes. You still look those pitches over and find the one you want. Gene Woodling used to swear he *never* got a hit without at least one strike on him. There is no need to panic at a single strike. It is often good practice to take a look at what the pitcher has to offer.

And a pitcher should not go all sulky and solemn when he gives up a long blow. Instead he should begin immediately to think of what he will do with the next guy. Does he like a pitch on the outside? How do you set him up for the "out" pitch? Is the low curve working well enough to count on? What did we decide about this guy before the game? That sort of thing goes through the mind of a real thinking pitcher, even after he has watched his good curve go flying into the upper stands.

While we are on the subject of thinking, let me recall the time when a lot of fans were laughing because Yogi was reported to have said that he could not "hit and think too." I doubt if Yogi put it just that way. But odd as it sounds, it is true that you can't take much time for actual thinking at the plate. That is, you cannot stand there and cogitate. Your reactions must be instinctive. If you get a notion, or a sign, that the fast ball is coming, you have only time to let fly at it with all your power. The reaction has to be quick as a snake's. You don't have time to put it into words: "Here comes a fast ball. I'd better get ready to swing." Your thinking has to be done before you get to the plate, or in between pitches, as you take a sign from the coach. A good crafty hitter, of the Nellie Fox, Ron Hunt, or Luis Aparicio type—a type I never pretended to be—will even react instinctively to a move by an infielder that leaves an opening where a safe hit can be poked through. Instinctive reactions of this sort come from practice, *serious* practice that is concerned with developing your natural skills and overcoming your weaknesses, and from concentration.

Concentration is not really the same as thinking. You concentrate at the plate and on the mound, even when you are not consciously making plans for your next move. If you are batting, you get your eye on the ball and sight it right down the bat when you swing, so you can even imagine you see it hit the bat. You close your mind to the noise from the stands or the heckling from the enemy bench. You are up there to hit and you look for the pitch you can hit best. Of course, in the big leagues pitchers are not about to serve you up the pitch they know you can put out of the park, so there has to be more than one pitch you can handle. But you have to have your eye fixed on the ball, so you can see just where it is coming, and your body must be so trained through practice that you will not chase bad pitches—or if you do start after them, you will not swing all the way. Even in batting practice you must employ this kind of concentration. And in batting practice you must make a point of leaving the bad pitches alone. You don't want your reflexes to get into bad habits.

A pitcher concentrates by working out the proper strategy for each new batter and by deciding, from pitch to pitch, with the help of the catcher, just how best to get this guy out of there without damage. Each batter, to a pitcher, is like a new problem to a mathematician or an accountant or a lawyer.

It requires him to recall all he knows about this particular ballplayer, and all that may have been said about him at the strategy meeting that dealt with this particular club. It may even require a conference with his catcher, to make sure they both know all the facts about this problem. The pitcher has control of the baseball, so he can set the pace of the performance. Especially if a batter, like most batters, is impatient to hit, the pitcher will do well to deliberate a bit. How can we make this guy hit the get-him-out pitch? What can we offer him that he is likely to go after but not so likely to hit safely? If he is noted for taking the first pitch, should we first feed him the second-best pitch right in the strike zone, to get ahead of him without showing him the best?

Outfielders concentrate by expecting every ball to come their way and by considering all the possibilities. Is there anybody in scoring position? Where is this batter's power—center, left, right? Where will I throw after the catch? Some outfielders like to get a sign from the shortstop, telling them what the pitch will be, so that they can shift into the proper area. A fast ball will come straight off the bat, while a curve is more likely to be hit a shade toward the "opposite" field, and the outfielder, knowing which is which, can sometimes be moving in time to anticipate a blow that he might otherwise have missed. It is more important, however, for an outfielder to know the habits of the hitters and to look for each hitter to drive a ball into the outfield. A man can grow pretty detached far out on the grass in the sleepy sun and you have to make sure you know the number of outs, what bases are occupied, the score, the inning, and the count on the batter. Otherwise you may find yourself, as more than one big leaguer has, catching a fly for out number two and trotting in toward the bench, thinking the side had been retired.

In the infield there is more pressure and it is more natural to concentrate on the upcoming play. But there must be physical concentration as well. You have to stay "on your toes." This does not mean perched on your tiptoes at all times. It means simply keeping your weight forward, ready to move in at every pitch, and expecting the ball to come straight at you. Big league infielders do not play straight up. Clete Boyer, one of the best glove-men in the league, crouches low with every pitch, so his chin is not much higher than his knees and his hands are almost scraping the ground. If a ball is rocketed at him, he is always ready. He does not have to bend over or reach down. He is right there, looking for the ball every second.

As a matter of fact, you have to learn to bend your knees in baseball. Not only does an infielder have to bend both knees and back to get down to where he can field the ball, but a pitcher has to bend his knees to get full power into his pitches. A pitcher who does not bend his knees as he pushes off from the ground is not getting his legs into the pitch. And a pitcher who lands straight up is not getting his back into it. When a catcher or a manager observes that his pitcher is failing to bend his back, he knows that it is time to send a signal to the bull pen. A fast-ball pitcher, like Jim Bunning, takes a longer stride than a man who depends on his curve—a pitcher like Whitey Ford for instance—and so he may not be able to land on his toes, as he should. But he will bend his knee as he gets ready to shove off from the mound. And probably if Jim had developed the habit of landing with bent knee, he would not topple off the mound as often as he does on that follow-through.

But to get back to the infield, you will notice that second basemen and shortstops are often shifting position, not just to adjust to the habits of a certain batter, but to get ready for a possible play. If we had a fast man on first, Bobby Richardson would often "cheat" a little toward second base, so he would not have so far to run to make a play there. Of course, this left a little more room for a man to poke through a hit, but Bobby would still be ready to move to his left, as he could do as well as anyone in the business. When a bunt was anticipated, Bobby might cheat a bit the other way, ready to cover first as Joe Pepitone charged the plate.

Third baseman and first baseman both, as well as the pitcher, must move in fast when a bunt is expected. There is no need to concede the success of a sacrifice. If the ball can be snatched up and fired to second (or third) for a force play, killing off the lead runner, there is an immense tactical and psychological advantage. You don't ever want to give up on any kind of ball, even an overthrow. If you can pounce on the ball and get it back, you can often help yourself to an out.

In the outfield it is even more important never to give up on a ball as long as it is in play. Even if you know you cannot make the catch, or feel sure you cannot, you can still start after the ball at once and tell yourself where you are going to throw the ball as soon as you retrieve it. Sometimes you will even catch a ball that you may not seem to have a chance for. There was a game at the Stadium some years ago in which I caught a ball I had no right to reach. I caught it because I kept after it, even though I knew it was past me. Hank Bauer was pursuing it too, and he could not catch it. But he slapped it with his glove so that it bounced off and struck me right on the chest. I hugged it for the out. And Bob Turley, who was pitching and who thought he had just blown the ball game, could have come out and hugged us both.

Outfielders not only learn to help each other in this way but they must keep talking to each other, so that they don't collide, or make a shoestring attempt on a ball that the other man could have caught easily. In the infield the fielders will often signal to each other, noiselessly, to indicate who will cover the bag on a certain play. Or the catcher may call everyone together to make sure each one knows who is going to cover the bag and who is going to charge for the bunt.

When you snatch up a bunted ball, there will always be someone to tell you what base to throw to. But the man who picks up the ball must really make the decision and make it in a split second—should he try for the lead runner or make the sure out at first? Don't just slam the ball to second because you hear someone shouting, "Second base!" Look there and be sure there is someone to take the throw, and see for yourself if you have a chance of getting the ball there ahead of the runner. In a pressure play of this type you don't have time to "think," in the sense of putting all the facts together and working out a solution. Whether you are infielder, catcher, or pitcher, you must have thought the possibilities of the play out beforehand, and you must react with ferocious speed. And you do that only when you are truly concentrating—giving all your attention to your job.

A lack of true concentration often leads to errors. Concentration by a fielder includes getting the head down and fixing the eye on a ground ball without fretting about what a bad bounce may do to you and without trying to give half your attention to the base-runner. Double plays, in amateur ball, are most often missed because the fielder, having watched the ball *almost* into his glove, lifts his head to see where he is going to throw the ball. In that last fraction of a second the ball may take a sudden eccentric bounce, or may skitter along the ground without any bounce at all. If the eyes are fixed on the ball, the hands will adjust automatically, and immediately. You certainly don't *think:* Oops! A bad bounce! I've got to raise my hands. But that does not mean you are not using your brains. The brain reacts instinctively to the training you have given it and it signals the muscles before you have half a chance to "think" about what you are doing.

There is such a thing as altogether too much thinking in baseball. When I got into my first slump, I just thought myself in deeper, trying to figure out all the things I might have been doing wrong and all the different ways I might adopt to correct these faults. You do have to use your head, of course, to figure out sometimes what has happened to your swing, or, if you are a pitcher, what has caused you suddenly to go wild high, or lose some of your quickness. But if you get to the point of brooding and fretting, checking yourself every time you go to the bat or to the mound and changing your whole battle plan with every pitch, then you can get wound up so your slump gets deeper and deeper. This sort of thinking can affect your confidence, which is your chief asset.

It is the same way with pressure. You need pressure, as I pointed out, to bring out the last ounce of effort. The pressure of a tight race has good effects as well as bad, for it can inspire you to accomplish near-miracles on the field or at bat. When I think of the value of pressure, I often recall what Sandy Amoros did to us in the sixth inning of the final game of the 1955 World Series. Sandy, a left-hander, had been sent to left field to replace Jim Gilliam, who had been shifted to second base. Billy Martin opened the inning by walking on four straight balls. Gil McDougald then crossed up the Dodgers by bunting, although we were two runs behind. Next up was Yogi Berra. Young Sandy shifted well over toward center field because Yogi generally hit to right. This time, however, Yogi sliced one about a foot inside the left-field foul line. Anybody looking at that ball just knew it was not going to be caught, especially with the outfielder so far out of position. But Sandy seemed to take off like a jet. While Billy and Gil just dug for home plate, figuring the ball was going to be out there a long, long time, Sandy headed straight for the stands. Fortunately for the Dodgers, he wore his glove on his right hand. He stuck his right hand out at the final second, gave an extra lunge, and plucked that ball out of the air close up against the rail. Gil was already partway to third base, and the relay doubled him (off first base) when he was still about ninety feet away. Billy luckily got back to second, because he had not moved quite so fast. Efforts like this always seem to pop up in the World Series. It is the extra pressure that makes ballplayers sometimes accomplish things that would ordinarily be far beyond their capacities.

But there is another sort of pressure that can wear you down and put lead in your heels. That is the pressure you put on yourself when you start to take your errors home with you at night and chew them over when you should be sleeping. It is the pressure that comes from having big ears, from hearing all the insults from the stands and reacting to all the boos. Just how you cope with this, I am not sure. You just grow up, or you learn to live with it. I know once I was watching Roger Maris when he was suffering intensely from this sort of thing, was allowing it to distract him from what was happening on the field and causing him to forget to run out ground balls, because he was too busy berating himself. I turned to Hank Bauer then and said, "Was I ever like that?"

"You sure were!" said Hank. And there was something about the way he said it that made me suspect that I was even worse.

Some pitchers duck this sort of pressure by taking care never to read the papers the day after they have lost a game.

Then there is Old Satchel Paige's famous advice: "Don't look behind. Something may be gaining on you!" I think however that how you deal with it depends a lot on your own make-up. There are athletes who are at their best when they are angered, because their anger is always directed at the opponent, or at the obstacle that got in their way. Billy Martin was like that. When he went to the plate angry, he was likely to put a pitch into the stands. But if you are inclined as I was to turn your anger against yourself, you have to practice mental relaxation—getting away from baseball and concentrating on having a good time, or on golf, or just on goofing off in the sun. Golf, of course, is a game that can tie you in knots too, for it is full of frustrations. But fishing or hunting, well, in those sports I can relax completely, being a country boy at heart.

Some pressures are wholly imaginary and can often be dispelled by just looking at your troubles in the light of calm logic. You take, for instance, this matter of pinch-hitting. I know there are some hitters who intensely dislike the pinch-hitting job because they feel they are always going to bat under pressure. But actually, this is not true at all. The hitter may feel he is on a spot and must deliver, or else. But when a man comes to bat in a pinch, the pinch is usually on the pitcher. There are probably men on base, threatening to score. If the pinch-hitter hits, the pitcher may be sent to the showers. If there is any pressure in these circumstances, it is felt by the pitcher and when the pitcher feels pressure, you have a special advantage over him. He knows he can't get fancy with you, probably cannot afford to "pitch around" you and take a chance on your walking, and knows too that you are up there because you can hit. So you have a head start in the contest, with a much better chance of forcing him to deliver the pitch you want.

The really experienced pinch-hitters, men like Smoky Burgess, if there is anybody else like him, go up to the plate just as relaxed as if they had been called to lunch. They don't lunge at the ball, don't flail at bad pitches. They know they can wait for what they want, and that if they don't get it, they'll very likely get a free ticket to first, with no time at bat, and not even the bother of running the bases, because there'll be a speedster to come in to do that. When the pressure is on the enemy, you can afford to stay loose.

Staying loose, however, does not mean any loss of concentration. You are just quietly confident, positive that you are in command of the situation, and sure that nothing is going to happen you won't be able to deal with. No one is ever any looser at the plate than Smoky Burgess, nor any more confident. And they say about Henry Aaron that he takes a nap between pitches, he is so beautifully relaxed. But don't ever believe that Hank is *really* asleep. Try to slip a good pitch by him, and he will belt it clear out of sight. He is more like the big cat, who is relaxed, even absent-looking, but who will strike with the speed of a bullet if his breakfast walks by.

This is the attitude Casey wanted us to cultivate when he urged us to stay loose. He did not mean we should clown it up. He just meant we should stay confident and relaxed, and not allow ourselves to imagine that one strike-out was going to end the season for us. So taking the game seriously and staying loose are not contradictory. You can be serious in your intent and relaxed in your attitude.

This relaxed attitude can carry over into your life off the diamond and make your relationships with other people much more pleasant. You begin to concern yourself less with your own worries and to recognize that other people may have burdens too. I suppose every professional athlete has to be self-centered to a certain degree. He does need to involve himself more than the non-athlete does in the development of his own physique and the proper exploitation of it. And in the scramble you do often have to push your way to the front or else get stepped on. But once you learn to relax with yourself, you discover that there are other people who may have suffered from shyness, or made dumb mistakes, or uttered foolish remarks they wish they could rub out. And you find out there is satisfaction in helping some kid grow up in his attitude toward his job and toward other members of the club. You find out sometimes that what seems like conceit is really just a protective front a kid may put up to keep people from finding out how scared and inadequate he really is.

It took me a long time to become at ease with the outside world, and I don't know as I am completely so even now. But I have discovered how to make allowances for myself as well as for others, and I have learned to feel, with complete sincerity, that a yell of encouragement, a really interested question from a fan, or a cheerful greeting, more than makes up for the boos offered by others—who really mean no harm at all but are just participating in their own way in the ball game. I discovered that even sportswriters were human, that they had to work under pressure too, and that they were not always out to make a bum out of a ballplayer just for the sports-page mileage they might develop. I was even able to grant that some of the harsh criticism they made of me might have had some basis in fact—a misunderstood fact usually, but still a fact. I realized that when I gave a guy a short answer—as I did one day in Boston—he heard only the short answer and may have had no idea of the pressure that kept me from taking the time to answer him in full.

Considering the other fellow's point of view this way is self-expanding. The first thing you know, you are applying it to all your life outside baseball, with the people you run up against in just moving through the world—the waiters, the cab drivers, the doormen, the ticket takers, and all the people who do or say things that might irritate you. You know that any one of them may have a private gripe, may have some woe at home you have no idea about, may be off his feed, or nervous, or scared, or sore about some insult he has taken, or mad at himself and the world just the way a young ballplayer used to be when he struck out three times in a row. (And believe me, if anyone can strike out three times in a row, I'm the man that knows how.)

Once you have learned to take life this way, your whole daily faring can become easier and happier. You lose the feeling that the world is full of guys who are out to put you down, or to ride on your back. You get rid of that desperation that can overcome you sometimes when you think your foot is slipping on the ladder rung. The sensation is like finally discovering you are a member of the club, only it is a lot bigger club than you could ever fit into the locker room at the Stadium.

chapter five

So here I am in, well, if not the twilight, at least the late afternoon of my baseball career, preparing to learn the one job in baseball I never even fooled around at—playing first base. At this writing (spring 1967) I feel pretty sure I can do the job well enough to avoid making a fool of myself in public. By the time this book comes out I may feel quite differently. But there are a few things about it I do know at this point: I have seen a few guys playing that position who just have to be worse than I am going to be; I intend to give it a good hard try; and I don't for a minute admit that it is going to be as great a strain on me physically as some writers have predicted.

Besides, I don't believe the club will suffer too much if I prove unable to qualify as the regular first baseman. The Yankees already have one of the best first basemen in the game—Joe Pepitone. They also have Mike Hegan, who can perform in big league style around first base too.

I will not be the first outfielder who has tried to play there for the sake of staying in the line-up. Babe Ruth played first for a while, late in his career, and they say he did poorly, even though he had been a first baseman years before, with the Red Sox as well as the Yankees. But Babe was going on thirty-eight when he took the job, and he was not looking his best at any position. He too had a trick knee that sometimes gave out on him. Joe

DiMaggio was a first baseman for one game and came out of the experience alive, without having made an error, although it left his nerves so jangled he never would try it again. But Joe was thrown in there with only a week to get used to the position.

I prefer to think about Tommy Henrich, who made the switch from the outfield to first base after he had played several seasons with the Yankees, and Johnny Mize, who kept on playing first base when he was past forty. Harmon Killebrew too had played a number of seasons in the majors before he made the switch to first. And when Stan Musial first tried the job, he led the league in errors in that position, and still became expert at it. Paul Waner played first base in the minors at the age of forty-three. And Nellie Fox tried it for Houston when he was thirty-eight. So I don't feel that I am too old, or too set in the ways of an outfielder, to make the shift.

I have discovered that sudden stops and turns, such as you make in playing any base, are no tougher on my knees than what I have been up against in the outfield. I find there is far less running and this may ease the strain a bit. As near as I can discover, my left knee is in good shape anyway. My right knee just cannot get any worse. Practically all the cartilage—the gristly stuff that acts as cushion between the joints—is gone anyway, so I don't see how I can do it any additional damage. My shoulder is all well and my hands are as good as ever. I can throw and I can stretch. Perhaps I cannot charge a bunt the way Joe Pepitone does. His hair is prettier too. But I can move in as well as most guys my age. As for my holding back, however, and not scrambling for ground balls out of my reach, that just cannot be. If a ball comes my way, I am going to try for it, if I break both legs in the process. That urge is built into me and will not be cured until they take my uniform away from me and lock it up.

As to my hitting, I am full of confidence. In 1966 I had one streak of eleven home runs in fourteen games, and I never in my life hit at a hotter pace than that. If I can hold somewhere near that for even part of the season, I am going to pay my way.

Baseball, it is true, has changed, and in some respects has got tougher than when I started. Pitching especially is meaner. It used to be absolutely standard, on a 3 and 0 count, for the pitcher to come in with a fast ball. If the coach turned me loose on that one, I did not have to doubt for a moment what was going to be thrown. But now these tough youngsters, in Baltimore, in Cleveland, and, yes, in Boston and Kansas City and everywhere else, are likely to throw you anything for a 3 and 0 pitch—a curve, a slider, even a change-up. They just must work harder on control. Or else, with the heavy stress nowadays on relief pitching, they don't need to pace themselves quite so carefully and can come in with the big pitch whenever they please.

Those Baltimore kids, Dave McNally and Jim Palmer especially, were brought up to give a batter fits. They will just never ease up on you. McNally, who has just about the best curve ball in the league, will throw that curve any time, no matter what the situation. You'd think every game was a World Series game with the score 1 to 0. And Wally Bunker of Baltimore has one of those sinkers you can break your back on, and he'll sling *that* at you when you might think he wouldn't dare try. That's one thing that keeps you from coasting in this game: the way these young pitchers keep popping up just when you have the old ones fairly well figured. There's Sam McDowell in Cleveland, who will wheel that ball in so fast sometimes it looks like a shirt button. In Kansas City they have Lew Krausse. And up in Boston there's Jim Lonborg, who is as tall as Radatz, even if not so big around. In Detroit they have Denny McLain, Lou Boudreau's son-in-law, who acts just as if he wanted to strike you out every time.

So far I have managed to hold my own with these boys and if I can stay all glued together this season, I don't doubt I'll still be able to get my share against them. It would be a relief, however, if they would cut off the flow of these kids for a while. They seem to be getting bigger and stronger every season.

Of course, we have some big strong boys too and some hitters that any pitcher could easily learn to dislike. If we can reverse a few of those one-run decisions, we can vault several places in the standing. I do not feel, on that account, that I enlisted in a lost cause when I signed on for another season. There are a few private ambitions I would like to realize—playing in the most games as a Yankee, hitting over 500 home runs. But most of all I would like once more to be on a winning club, and I don't believe that ambition is unattainable, no matter what the professional thinkers-out-loud may say.

There are of course a few aspects of organized baseball that do not entirely suit me. I think the scheduling is too tough, that we play too many games too close together. It is bad for the players, bad for the fans, and bad for baseball for a club to take the field too woozy from lack of sleep and time changes to care whether they win or lose. Of course that TV money makes the top salaries possible and it is going to be hard to forgo. Now when you drop a few night games, you drop whole buckets full of TV cash, and even the lowest-paid player is going to feel a few pangs at sacrificing that, because that's where he hopes his next big raise is coming from.

It would please me too if players and management could find some way to decide on salaries without these no-holds-barred salary negotiations that are played up in the press occasionally until both players and management are made to look unpleasantly greedy to the fans. I recognize that these offers and counter-offers and "final" salary figures are legitimate bargaining devices. I know too that management has to have some protection against contract jumping and competitive bidding. But a young player does not have much leverage in one of these salary sessions and I am afraid they may sometimes wind up with a fellow getting so much less than he deserves that he cannot give the game the wholehearted devotion he needs to.

But the few gripes I have against baseball are trivial indeed when set against the many advantages it has given me. It has built me a whole new world to live in and provided comforts, education, and associations for my kids that would have been far out of sight for a miner's family. Still, I am just one guy out of a few hundred who made it to the top. There are hundreds of others in the game who never won a share of the richest rewards, and who yet helped us win ball games and who never held back an ounce when the game was on. I feel a deep obligation to those fellows and I hope a way will be found for all of them to share in some way in the prosperity that all organized sport now enjoys.

There have been guys who face the prospect of leaving the game without any show of regret, who feel, or pretend to feel, a sense of relief at getting away from the pressure of the interviewers, the autograph seekers, and the frantic fans who sometimes act as if you had no right to a life of your own. And it is fashionable to put down this whole idea of being a public figure, of being recognized in restaurants and on the street, of having to cope with requests to kick in time to help somebody's pet charity. But if I said I really dislike this sort of thing, I'd be a hypocrite. It is true that there are pests who can prod you pretty near to violence, when they whack you on the back in a tavern and spill your drink into your lap, or move in on you in a restaurant and wear out your ear with their own notions of how long-dead ball games might have been won. But most fans are considerate and would like nothing better than to find an excuse to do you a personal kindness. You can work out ways of dodging the pests, and the few irritations that do arise are a very small price to pay for the advantages that accrue. Perhaps somebody does spot you in traffic and tie up the street while he runs over to ask you to sign something. But it is also true, in places where I am known, like Dallas or New York, that parking my car is never the drag to me that it is to most people. Maybe if you go into a night club, there will be people to slow you down as you try to get to your table, or who will interrupt your conversation to tell you hello. But being able to walk into such a place without a reservation and have the captain make a place for you and your crowd more than makes up for that.

So I am not eager at all to say good-bye to baseball. I am playing for the best manager in the world and I think our club is still strong enough to win more games than it loses. And as long as it wins, and I can contribute something to winning, I want to be a part of it. I can wrap my bad knee up now so that the discomfort is almost negligible, unless the game lasts unusually long. And the rest of me feels strong enough to play in every game. To stay up in the pennant race, a club has to get good seasons out of all its players at once, especially its pitchers. We have pitchers who, when they are at their best, are the equal of any, and some that are better than most. If Whitey Ford's arm comes back strong; if Al Downing turns in the kind of season I know he is capable of; if Mel Stottlemyre just pitches like Mel Stottlemyre and Jim Bouton gets his warmup system straightened out, then there are not too many clubs that are going to be ahead of us. Some of our hitters have had bad years. But you can't tell me they have forgotten to hit. Elston Howard is still able to put a ball in the left-field stands. And Joe Pepitone could be the best center fielder in the league. The only really doubtful spot I can see is first base. And privately I think I am in for a real good year—at the plate if not in the field.

This is not conceit on my part. It is just confidence. When I am free from aches and pains, I feel capable of hitting baseballs just as hard and just as far as I ever did. The way to tell if you are beginning to fade at the plate is to check where the hits are dropping. If you are slicing them all, not getting around on the good pitches any more, not hitting them up your own power alley, then you know that your rocking-chair days are drawing nigh. But I am still getting good wood on the baseball and when I hit them they still go mostly into center field, either to the left or right, depending on which side of the plate I am standing on. This may sound like a brag, but it is just an observation.

If I ever do get tempted to brag, or to dwell on the great deeds I have performed, I have a scene I can recall that will bring me right back to the hard ground. It was a number of years ago this happened. It may have been one of my real good years. I don't recall exactly. But it was surely not one of my good days. In four at bats I had struck out three times, blowing several chances to win the game for the Yankees. After the loss I was the gloomiest man in the locker room and I undressed slowly. My chin was very nearly in my lap as I reluctantly pulled my stockings off, silently calling myself names.

One of my favorite teammates had brought his little boy into the clubhouse and the kid was wandering there, staring at the players with those oversize eyes kids have. Suddenly I realized the boy was right at my shoulder, watching me steadily. I looked up at him and he returned my glance very solemnly. I felt sure I knew just what he was going to say: "Cheer up. Hang in there. You'll be okay." I managed half a smile and got ready to accept his encouragement. Then without changing his expression, in a perfectly level voice, with his eyes fixed intently on mine, he spoke two words: "You stink!"

And that was just what I had been telling myself. Fortunately, I never really believed it.

LESSON FIVE

As no one knows better than I, there is much to learn about playing first base that is different from what must be learned to play the other infield positions. The first baseman is the target for almost as many throws as the catcher and he must always expect a throw to be off target. If you set yourself, when you are playing first, only to get good throws, you are not going to be able to adjust for the bad ones.

The very first lesson a first baseman has to learn is to get to the base fast. Don't make the fielder wait until you get there. Even if it is going to be a routine put-out, move to the bag in a hurry, and be there ready to take the throw as soon as the fielder has the ball. The correct position is to be standing on the second-base side of your base, with your feet just about touching the bag. Take a look at the bag before the throw comes, so you will know just where it is in relation to your feet. Then keep your eye on the man who is fielding the ball.

The first baseman stretches for a throw so he will get the ball a fraction of a second sooner and thus beat the runner. But you should not stretch until you see the ball is on its way to you. Stand there, with your knees slightly bent, ready to move after the ball in any direction. If the throw is delayed, then you have got to really stretch to meet it, just as far as you can reach. If you are right-handed, you put your right foot on the bag, so you can take a full stride with your left leg and get that glove out as far as it will go. If you have glanced at the bag ahead of time, you won't have to take your eye off the ball to go looking for the bag. Put your toe right on the bag—not just your heel, or your stretch may pull it off. But be careful to leave at least half of the bag for the runner or he may put his spikes right into your foot.

Often a fast throw is low. If it is, you have to play it like a ground ball, bending right over to field it out in front of your feet, and to dig it out of the ground. Bend your knees and bend your back to get down there and get your head right over the ball.

If the throw is high, you may be able to reach it by just backing off, keeping your right foot on the bag, and stepping into foul territory with your left foot. This will allow the throw to travel a little further and may give it a chance to come down within reach. Of course, if the throw is far off target, you are going to have to leave the bag to field it. It is more important to keep the ball from getting by you than it is to keep your foot on the base, and sometimes you can retrieve the ball and still get back to the bag in time for the out. If the ball is off target toward the inside of the bag, then you may be able to slap the ball on the runner as he goes by.

Probably the toughest throw to handle is the one that seems to be headed right for the runner. This is the play where you need plenty of confidence, for you must sometimes pick that throw right off the runner's chest. Do not try to take this throw in foul ground. Get it in front of the runner and if you are off the base, swing your glove back to make the tag.

When there is no runner on first, the first baseman has to play back and be ready for ground balls, just like any other infielder. There is no boundary line for him. Anything he can reach is his, and if it pulls him too far off the bag, the pitcher has the job of covering to make the out. This is the kind of play that some people think may give me trouble and on which some advisers say I should cut down my range. Well, that I am just not able to promise to do. If any ground balls come within reaching distance of me, I know I am going to try to field them and I hope to make a few assists as well as put-outs at this position. There are pop-flies to take care of too, often into short right field, or in foul territory off toward the stands. There are often other players trying for the same ball, usually the second baseman and the right fielder, and you have to be ready to give way if one of the others has a good crack at it. Actually you are not in the best position to get the balls hit over your head. But that does not mean you should not try for them, if they are out of reach of the others.

Because the first baseman's glove is like a net that you carry in your hand, many players like to make these catches with one hand and I don't see anything wrong with that. Joe Pepitone manages that very well and he is one of the top glove men in that position. But I think it is a good idea to make the catch relatively high—near eye level, so that if the ball pops out, you may have another grab at it before it hits the ground.

When you make a throw to the pitcher covering the bag, don't rifle it at him. He will be coming full tilt for the bag and you have got to let him meet the ball on the way. You throw to the *pitcher* and not to the bag. That is, you try to time your throw so he can take it before he gets to the base. Otherwise, if he has to concentrate on getting the ball, he may miss the bag. Allow him two or three steps before he reaches the bag, and then he will be able to spot the bag and get his foot on it after he has the ball. The best kind of throw to use is a soft underhand toss. And remember what I said about throwing the ball on the double play: Don't conceal the ball behind your glove or arm. Face the pitcher directly and move toward him, with your glove pulled out of the way, as you toss the ball.

Another part of the job at first base that I expect may give me a little trouble is fielding bunts. When a sacrifice is obvious, the first baseman has to charge toward the plate, in the hope of picking the ball up soon enough to get the lead runner. You start your charge just as soon as the batter moves into bunting position and you keep your eye on him. When you get the ball, always take a look at the lead runner, usually at second but sometimes at third, and see if you have a chance for him. If you have, fire the ball hard, right at the bag—provided there is someone there to take the throw. If you haven't, get the ball to first, where the second baseman will be covering. This is a play where you have to make the decision as to whether there is a play or not. Don't hesitate about it, or it may be too late to make any play at all. If you think you have a chance to get the lead runner, don't fake or delay. Get that throw off fast. A right-handed player will not be in a position on the first-base line, after fielding a bunt, to make the throw to second smoothly. He may find himself twisting his body halfway back to get into position to throw hard. It is probably better on this play to turn all the way around to your left and let fly as you face second base. This will make your throw more accurate and the slight extra split second will be compensated for by the added speed of the throw. The throw should go to the second baseman inside the baseline, so it won't cross the path of the runner, or permit the runner to block off the second baseman's view of the ball.

In holding a runner on the bag, a first baseman has to take care not to get between the runner and the base. He has no right to block off the runner, so he should stand on the inside corner of the base, toward the plate, and keep his glove always ready to make a target for the pitcher. Be sure you stay right there until the ball is on the way to the plate. Then get back into fielding position. Don't let your own pitcher fool you with his move. I have seen that happen in the big leagues, when a pitcher has a really deceptive move, so that the first baseman had already moved back into fielding position before the pitcher has fired the pick-off throw. Then the pitcher has to go through with the throw, even to the baseman far off the bag, or he is guilty of a balk.

When the throw comes to you, you should turn toward the runner to put the tag on him. Don't turn to your left and swing that glove down behind you without looking. Sometimes a first baseman does that and finds nobody there! The runner may have already taken off for second. So turn to the right with the ball and get it right down on the bag, where the runner must slide into it. If you have time to hop into position straddling the bag you will be in the best position to tag the man out. But if you can't do that, just take care not to be blocking the baseline without the ball. Stay on the home-plate corner of the bag until you have the ball in your glove.

The picture play at first base is one that I don't expect to be making too often. That is what is known as the 3-6-3 double play, when the first baseman, with a man on first, fields a ground ball and fires it to second for the force before he makes the out at first—then hustles back to the bag in time to take the return throw that puts the hitter out.

This is a play that takes plenty of hustle and usually will not work if you have a really fast man coming down to first. But if the ball is hit hard and gets to you quickly, and the runner has not started with the pitch, you can make this play by scrambling. Just be sure you face second base when you throw, and keep the throw off the baseline, then sprint for your own base and be there, knees bent and arms relaxed, ready for any kind of return throw.

On pop-flies in the infield, let the pitcher or catcher captain the play and tell you if you can have the ball. But on any other kind of ball take whatever you can reach. Sometimes the pitcher will make a stab at a ball as he runs to his left to cover first base. If it gets by him, you must be there to nail it, because he will keep right on going toward the base and you should try to feed him the ball before he gets there. But if you see that you can make the play yourself by beating the runner to the bag, go ahead and do it. The less you make the pitcher run the longer he'll last, and the fewer throws you make the fewer chances there will be for an error.

As no one knows better than I, just studying what to do at first base or even learning it all by heart is still a few hundred yards away from actually playing the position. Because plays develop so fast around that bag, you have to practice and practice, until your reactions become automatic. It is a good idea, wherever you practice, to have a base to work around, even if you just draw a square in the dirt. The best skill you can develop is an instinctive feeling for where the bag is as you make a play. And remember always to look for that bag and *know* where it is in relation to your feet *before* you take the throw.

One of the first baseman's most important jobs is acting as cutoff man on throws from the outfield. This means that you have to be the one to intercept a throw to the plate and try to nail a runner at second or third. To do this properly you have to back up away from the bag so you can get the whole diamond in view. If you stand too close to first base, you are not going to be able to see the base-runner and so you will have to waste time looking for him after you get the ball. So move a few yards back toward home and be ready—if the catcher calls, "Cut it off!"—to grab the throw and rifle it to the base the runner is headed for. Of course, if the catcher yells, "Let it go!" you do just that, because it is more important to get that man who is trying to score. It is up to the outfielder to keep his throw low enough so you can reach it without a ladder.

Now we have covered, if not everything I know about baseball, at least most of the important points, as far as I am able to express them. There are many bits of technique and details of tactics that can be learned only by playing the game, which is how I learned. In athletics no lesson is really learned just through understanding it. You have to be able to do it. Your muscles have to be trained along with your mind, and that means conditioning and practice.

I have not gone into very fine detail on conditioning methods, because I think every man has his own pet methods that work best for him. I know my own strengths and weaknesses best, so well that I don't want anyone else to bandage up my bad knee. I believe that as long as you take care not to get flabby or overweight, and remember the need for fairly strenuous workouts every day, you can take the exercises that appeal to you most and perform them under the conditions that get the best results for you. I have already mentioned Jim Bouton's warmup methods, which are strictly his own. After discovering that it often took him a few innings to get his fast ball working, he developed his "double-warmup" plan, in which he throws for several imaginary innings a long time before the game begins, takes a breather, then starts his regular warmup before the game. That's his way of doing it. For someone else it might not work.

So we get back to one of the first points I made—that everybody has to develop his own best way of batting, throwing, and running the bases. And you develop these only by actually playing the game as often and as long as you are allowed.

There is really only one absolute essential. That is that you *enjoy* the game. If it is not fun to play, you'll never be any good at it, no matter how much expert coaching you receive. It is, after all, a game, and it was invented for enjoyment. It is, of course, most fun when you are on the winning side. And that is where I hope to be for a long time to come.

INDEX

K

L

M

N

O

P